THEY FLEW THE ATLANTIC

They Flew the Atlantic

by

Robert de la Croix

Translated from the French by

Edward Fitzgerald

W · W · NORTON & COMPANY · INC · New York

CONTENTS

ILLUSTRATIONS

AUTHOR'S PREFACE

ON October 11th, 1910, an epic opened up in man's conquest of his environment, an epic rich in extraordinary adventures and bright with great deeds of heroism and self-sacrifice. It was the aerial conquest of the Atlantic Ocean. On that day an airship took off from America to make the first air contact between the Old Continent and the New. But the attempt was technically premature, and the airship, or dirigible as it was called then, came down in the sea and was lost. Fortunately—though almost by a miracle—all the members of its crew were saved.

Before long came the First World War, and for over four years daring aviators had other things to think about. But in 1919, immediately after the war, their thoughts turned again at once to the challenge of the Atlantic—and this time their efforts met with greater success. A two-stage crossing from Newfoundland to the Azores, and from there to Portugal and on to England was made by Lieut.-Comdr. A. C. Read and his crew in a U.S. Navy hydroplane. And two weeks after that came the first direct crossing, from Newfoundland to Ireland, by Captain John Alcock and Lieut. Arthur W. Brown. Then, within a month, the British dirigible R-34, commanded by Major G. G. Scott, flew from Scotland to New York across the widest part of the Atlantic Ocean.

All these were heartening successes, but at the same time they showed that the task was no light one. Alcock and Brown managed to reach the West of Ireland only by the skin of their teeth; two of the three hydroplanes which started off under Lieut.-Comdr. Read came down in the sea; and the R-34 had to fight for four days against mist and contrary winds before finally reaching its destination—with very little fuel left.

There were no further direct flights until 1927, but that was a great year in the story of the air. On both sides of the Atlantic, airmen were getting their planes ready, and in the meantime, of course, air construction and design had greatly improved, so that machines were now available which could—theoretically at least—fly direct from one continent to the other without difficulty. But there was one condition, and an important one: the weather conditions had to be favourable. The meteorological reports were now carefully studied, and each party was anxious to be first.

Actually two Frenchmen, Nungesser and Coli, were the first to try, and on May 6th they took off from Le Bourget in their plane *L'Oiseau Blanc*. The soon left the coasts of France behind them and set out over the Atlantic—but nothing further was ever heard of them. Presumably they came down in the Atlantic. It was a set-back, and it showed indeed that although the Atlantic had been flown, it was not yet something that could be reckoned on with confidence. Nungesser and Coli failed, but their failure did not discourage the others, and about a fortnight later a young American airman named Charles A. Lindbergh took off to fly the Atlantic in the opposite direction in his monoplane *Spirit of Saint Louis*. In a perfect flight he linked New York and Paris in thirty-three hours.

For the sake of a headline irresponsible journalism tried to pin the description of 'The Flying Fool' on to him, but this was rubbish. On the contrary Charles Lindbergh prepared his flight with care and forethought, and he carried it out with the skill of a born navigator in the teeth of difficult weather conditions. That is why his flight was something more than a symbol of man's daring in face of the unknown. Like Byrd's subsequent transatlantic flight, which almost ended in disaster, it was a demonstration that the Atlantic could be flown even in poor weather.

In the same year, Chamberlin and Levine succeeded in flying across the Atlantic to Germany.

These three were the only successful transatlantic flights of 1927, though there were many attempts, some of which ended in disaster. Of those who lost their lives some were just unlucky, for they deserved to succeed. But others failed because they had not prepared their flights with sufficient care, and still others because they took irresponsible risks.

But the east–west crossing, the one Nungesser and Coli had tried, still remained to be flown by aeroplane. It was much more difficult and dangerous than the west–east crossing, because anyone attempting it would have to reckon with more or less constant contrary winds.

In 1928 a German airman named Hermann Koehl, accompanied by Baron Guenther von Huenefeld, flew from Germany to Ireland, and from there, accompanied by Major James C. Fitzmaurice of the Irish Free State Army, across the Atlantic. They crashed on Greenly Island, Newfoundland, and were lucky to escape with their lives, but they made the first east–west crossing.

In 1929 two Frenchmen named Lefèvre and Lotti flew the Atlantic from west to east, and in the same year Dieudonné Costes and Maurice Bellonte, also Frenchmen, took off to attempt the east–west flight, but were compelled to turn back. But in the following year, after a long and patient wait, they too succeeded in making the east–west crossing; this time from Paris to New York, and completely successfully. Their flight, like Lindbergh's, was a triumph of calculated audacity, careful preparation and a high degree of flying and navigational skill.

In 1932 Amelia Earhart flew from Harbour Grace in Newfoundland to Londonderry, demonstrating that women aviators could fly the Atlantic, no less than men.

In 1933 Maurice Rossi and Paul Codos flew from New York to Paris, and in the following year from Paris to New York.

Apart from these outstanding flights there were a series of minor successes and failures. Not all the latter ended tragically; for example the extraordinary adventure of Stanley Haussner, who was fished out of the sea after having drifted around on his plane for a week.

In the meantime airmen were no less active in the South Atlantic, and in 1922 the Portuguese airmen Captain Cabral and

Captain Coutinho flew from Lisbon to Brazil, a remarkable exploit for those days—though it was not a non-stop flight, and took them two months and was carried out in three different machines. After them came Franco, de Pinedo and Sarmiento de Beires, but their flights were still in stages, and it was not until 1927 that the Frenchman Dieudonné Costes and Joseph Le Brix crossed the South Atlantic in one non-stop flight. After that the same feat was performed by Italian, Spanish and Franco-Uruguayan crews.

In 1930 Mermoz made the first commercial crossing of the South Atlantic, using a hydroplane; and after that his numerous flights dominated the history of South Atlantic flying. In 1936 he disappeared without trace on a new flight, having made twenty-four successful previous crossings and thereby established himself as amongst the great airmen of his day.

In that same year experimental flights were being made across the North Atlantic with a view to inaugurating regular air services, such as the French and German air lines were already providing between Europe and Latin-America, and on July 5th, 1937, two hydroplanes made the first normal commercial crossings; the one from Ireland to Newfoundland, the other in the opposite direction.

With this, the period of pioneering Atlantic flight was over. The Atlantic was harnessed, and before long a regular service in each direction was being run by giant transatlantic air liners. The men who had set off at dawn in their small machines, never knowing whether they would arrive, had opened the way to them as surely as the great circumnavigators of the past had opened the way to the swift greyhounds of the oceans.

THEY FLEW THE ATLANTIC

I

First Attempt by Air

IT was 20.00 hours on October 15th, 1910. The helmsman of the *Bullard*, a four-masted barque, bound from Boston to Norfolk, had just taken the wheel to do his watch. The sea was heavy and the sky low, and suddenly, ahead of him and a little to starboard, he spotted a red light above the surface of the sea and moving slowly down on his ship.

He immediately called the skipper, and Captain Sawyer hurried up on to his bridge. Yes, there it was; a red light, as though suspended in the air, and quite unmistakable despite the heavy mist which was beginning to blanket everything. It was obviously a very big ship to have a red light at that height over the surface.

Captain Sawyer ordered the helm to be put over to port to avoid a collision with the stranger, and this was done. He continued to study the light through his glasses; the odd thing was that though on this altered course the stranger should now have been showing her green navigation light, the light was still red. Another queer thing was that although the captain could now see the sombre mass of the ship's superstructure through the mist, he could not see the hull.

'Sound the fog-horn,' he ordered; and the long moaning blare rolled over the ocean for thirty seconds, stopped, and started up intermittently.

'You can hear her engines now, sir,' said the helmsman. And it was true. When the fog-horn was silent you could distinctly hear them. Sailors were now lining the deck rails of the *Bullard* and staring over at the strange craft that was still approaching.

There was a good deal of excited speculation. Was the stranger a floating hulk? No, she couldn't be—because of the light. But why wasn't she showing her red and green navigation lights in their proper positions? And why, above all, did she keep on at collision course?

On the bridge the captain of the *Bullard* was already fearing for the safety of his ship, but then suddenly the mist opened up to reveal an extraordinary sight not more than a cable-length away. Above the surface of the sea floated a cigar-shaped object, and under it there was what looked like a lifeboat hanging in the air suspended from the cigar-shaped mass, while falling away from the mass and trailing in the sea was a hose-like line. The captain was the first to grasp the significance of what everyone could now see, and almost mechanically, with the instinct of the experienced seaman, he took the necessary steps to avoid a collision. He reckoned the airship's height at about a hundred feet, or hardly more than the masts of the *Bullard*, and he ordered calcium flares to be shown.

He could hear other voices now, besides the excited shouts of his own crew. But they came to him distorted through the mist. And then wild shouts went up from his own deck: 'It's crashing into the masts!' And so it certainly looked. The roar of the airship's engines was very loud now, and a breath of hot air enveloped the *Bullard* for a moment or two. But then the expected crash did not happen, and the airship passed either just above or just to the side of the masts.

Gradually it faded to the rear, remaining visible through the mist for perhaps five minutes, and then it was lost to view. On board the *Bullard* Captain Sawyer now had to reassure his crew, for some of them were superstitious men, and they feared they had seen some terrible apparition. It had been a dirigible all right, but that fact still left a good many others unexplained. What was it doing over the Atlantic with its nose directed towards Europe over three thousand miles away? No airship was capable of flying that distance across the ocean. No aeronaut would deliberately have attempted such an act of folly.

And yet one had. October 15th, 1910, was an outstanding date in the history of aviation, for on that day an aeronaut named Walter Wellman set out to do the impossible—to join the New World with the Old by air in his dirigible *America*.

Earlier that same day, at about eight o'clock in the morning, two motor-cars had driven on to the airfield at Atlantic City. In one of them a woman in tears was sitting beside a silent man of perhaps forty whose face was grave. Moored to a tall mast on the balloon station was an airship, and below it on the ground was a group of men, including its crew of five. The cars stopped a little way off, and their occupants walked across to the dirigible. It was ready to take off on the first transatlantic flight to Europe.

At first the announcement that the attempt would be made had not been taken seriously. First of all, the record long-distance flight by a dirigible was about six hundred miles at the time, and the distance across the Atlantic was more than five times as great. And secondly, Walter Wellman, the man who now proposed to make the attempt, had already disappointed public opinion on one occasion, when, having declared that he would fly over the North Pole to Spitzbergen, he had not even attempted to carry out his promise.

Despite this, however, crowds had put in an appearance at the airfield at Atlantic City to see the *America* set off on her flight. They had been disappointed; they had waited, but the dirigible had remained moored to its mast. The weather was unfavourable, they were told.

The newspapers now began to turn the thing into a joke. Wellman was a boaster; he would no more fly to Europe than he had flown over the Pole. He was a first-class publicity man, no doubt, but not much of an aeronaut. It wouldn't do to take him and his pretensions too seriously. So when Wellman announced, once again, that he was about to start, and fixed the date for October 15th, he was no longer taken seriously; when the time came no one was at the airfield except his crew and the men who were to help in getting her away. The *America* was 230 feet long, with a diameter of over 50 feet at her widest point, and she was powered by two 90 h.p. engines driving four air-screws. The Atlantic crossing was to take between four and ten days, depending on weather conditions.

'We are going to attempt to reach Europe by air across the Atlantic,' said Wellman. 'We think we have a good chance of success, but we know that it is a difficult and dangerous undertaking. However, it is not a foolhardy experiment, and we have done everything possible to ensure our success and our personal safety.'

What precautions had actually been taken? Well, for one thing the airship was equipped with wireless which would allow it to send out news of its progress to the world, and, if necessary, call on ocean-going liners for assistance. Also, it carried a lifeboat fastened beneath the gondola. In addition, the airship had a guide-rope, a kind of hose hanging below her, which also served as storage space for spare petrol. If the airship rose high in the air this guide-rope acted as ballast; when it flew lower the guide-rope trailed in the sea, which took part of the airship's weight.

Wellman now joined his men. They all knew that the flight would be difficult and dangerous, but they were not intimidated by the prospect, and Wellman had experienced no difficulty at all in obtaining a suitable crew. In fact, he had received almost a hundred offers from Britain, France, Germany and Russia, as well as from his own country, the United States. Out of all these volunteers he had chosen a crew of five. Three of these were mechanics: Vaniman, who was acting as his second-in-command, Loud and Aubert. The other two were the navigator, Simon, and the wireless operator, Irwin.

Wellman shook hands warmly with each of them. It was quite clear that he was anxious. He had been assured that weather conditions over the Atlantic were favourable, but there was a ground mist. The *America* was very heavy, too heavy perhaps—twelve and a half tons. But in agreement with his second-in-command he decided that they could not afford to lighten their load; they might well need all the fuel-oil and all the food they had on board.

The weeping woman was his wife, and his daughters were also there to see him off. Resolutely he embraced and kissed them good-bye and then joined his crew, who were already in the gondola of the *America*, one of them holding their mascot, the cat 'Kiddo'.

'Cast off,' he ordered, and the ropes holding the *America* sailed through the air to the ground, whereupon the vessel immediately rose by about a hundred feet. She was still attached to a small tug, and for about ten minutes the watchers saw her being towed out to sea. Then the tow-line was cast off too, and the *America* disappeared into the mist leaving the tug to put about and return to the shore.

In the gondola of the *America* Walter Wellman studied the chart spread out before him. His course was to go over Cape Breton and Newfoundland, where, from the Strait of Belle Isle, the Atlantic crossing proper would begin. A wireless message arrived. It was from the Special Correspondent of the *Daily Telegraph*, who wanted to know whether Wellman's first impressions had done anything to confirm his belief that he would be able to fly to Europe.

'We have only just started,' replied Wellman reasonably. 'It's much too soon to make prophecies.'

At dusk the steamer *Coamo* spotted the *America* flying about eighty miles out to sea, when according to plan she should have been at least two hundred miles out. What had happened to cause the delay?

Wellman had four and a half tons of fuel-oil on board, and as the engines consumed less than half a ton per day, this was sufficient for the maximum ten days the flight might last. Unfortunately, some of the fuel-oil was carried in the hose-like guide-rope, and this proved over-heavy, trailing down deep

into the sea, retarding the progress of the *America* and inter-
fering with her aerodynamic qualities. Further, the engines
were not giving as much power as Wellman had hoped. The
forward engine, which had eight cylinders and had been assembled by an expert who had come over specially from
France, was giving only about half what had been expected of
it, whilst the other engine, of four cylinders, had broken down
shortly after the start and had been out of action for half an
hour. By early evening the eight-cylinder engine seized up
altogether and they were unable to start it again.

'You could throw it overboard as ballast without any in-
convenience,' observed Vaniman drily.

But that wasn't the end of their troubles. With the coming of
night, the temperature dropped and the gas in the envelope
contracted, with the result that the *America* lost height. The
heavy guide-rope, whose weight had certainly been badly mis-
calculated in relation to the airship's buoyancy, sank deeper
into the sea; and with the increased drag speed diminished still
further. But Wellman's confidence was unshaken.

'That doesn't mean we can't get across,' he said. 'All we need
is favourable winds. The one engine will give us sufficient
speed to manœuvre.'

No one protested, and so the hopeless undertaking continued.

The cat noticed it first, and with its hair standing on end and
its tail as stiff as a poker it dived for safety into a bale of rope.
A stream of sparks from the exhaust of the one engine still in
operation shot ceaselessly along the gondola. For a moment the
human members of the crew were paralysed. The *America* was
filled with highly inflammable hydrogen gas, and in addition
she still had over four tons of equally highly inflammable fuel-
oil on board. At any moment she could be turned into a flying
torch, lighting up the deserted sea for a short while before
plunging into it.

'Switch off the engine, Vaniman,' shouted Wellman.

Vaniman obeyed at once. The throb of the engine ceased, and with it the shower of sparks. But at once they had to cope with a new difficulty: the *America* became out of control and began to drift helplessly. Wellman now had to choose between using the engine and risking a disaster by fire, or allowing himself to be driven off course by the wind and away from the shipping routes to an area where no help could be expected.

'Start her up again, Vaniman,' he ordered finally, 'but for heaven's sake see if you can do something about those exhaust sparks.'

Once again Vaniman obeyed; the trail of sparks re-appeared, but Wellman now navigated to keep the danger down to a minimum. He was keenly aware that their great adventure might come to a terrible end at any moment, but at least he would do his best. He and his companions were the first men to fly over the Atlantic, and they were the first to have been in wireless touch with the ground from a dirigible—and then unexpectedly they set up a new record: they became the first men in an airship to risk collision with a ship at sea! Wellman, who was at the helm, saw the danger at once, and he manœuvred coolly and skilfully to avoid collision with a four-masted vessel we know to have been the *Bullard*. His crew were not nearly so excited at the astonishing encounter as were the men on the deck of the *Bullard*—but to encounter a ship on the high seas was nothing extraordinary, whereas to encounter an airship at sea in those days very definitely was.

Towards dawn the stream of sparks from the exhaust grew definitely less dangerous. Wellman tried to estimate his position, calculating the drift, the course, the speed, the distance covered. But in the end he had to admit reluctantly that he didn't know exactly where they were. Owing to the weather he had not been able to take shots of either the sun or the stars since their take-off.

Then much shorter waves became visible below and indicated the near presence of land. It was Nantucket Island—they were not very far on their way as yet. An hour later the mist dispersed and they could see the horizon, but there was no sign of land. The Atlantic Ocean stretched away endlessly.

There was silence in the gondola of the *America* now. All of them knew by this time that it would be wise to give up. They had only one engine left, and that was the smaller of the two. It was neither powerful enough nor reliable enough, and it was already beginning to run very hot. The airship itself was too heavy, and the hose-like guide-rope was sinking deeper and deeper into the water, whereas according to calculations it should have done little more than skim along the surface. At the same time squalls were blowing up from the south-west, making the *America* oscillate, though so far she was keeping her course eastward towards Europe, over three thousand miles away. And beneath them a green sea streaked with white spume was rolling and pitching heavily.

No, the situation was not hopeful, and the prospects were not promising either. Wellman was even beginning to wonder whether he had the right to risk the lives of his men any further. For the moment they were still in the shipping lanes and if they had to come down it would be possible to launch the lifeboat and hope for rescue. But if he insisted on going on they might be blown off course, and then if they had to come down after all . . . In the end he called them together.

'You know the risks as well as I do,' he said bluntly. 'What do you think: should we go on or turn back?'

Vaniman was the only one who obviously thought that the best thing to do would be to turn back, but when the others voted in favour of going on he too agreed.

'Right,' said Wellman. 'We'll go on, then. In the meantime, fry us some eggs and bacon, Aubert. I'm as hungry as a hunter.'

'Any news of the *America*?'
'None.'
That summed up the gist of the constantly repeated dialogue going on between wireless stations all along the eastern sea-

board of the American continent, and between ships at sea. Nothing had been heard of the *America* since shortly after the start. Not that this was really alarming. For one thing the airship's transmitter was not very strong, and for another Wellman would be anxious to conserve his accumulators.

The news that he had actually started off on his flight across the Atlantic, after all, had at first aroused great enthusiasm, but before long this had given way to a more sober appraisal of his chances. No one with any expert knowledge put them very high.

Wireless operators everywhere within range tried to contact the *America*, but without success. There was no reply to their calls. And yet it was now growing more and more urgent that their signals should at least be heard, if not replied to, for a violent cyclone which had swept devastatingly over Cuba had now turned north, and it was calculated that within forty-eight hours at the outside it must cross the course of the *America*.

Seated at his apparatus with the earphones on, Irwin, the wireless operator of the *America*, jotted down the few messages and fragments of messages he was able to pick up. All the signals were weak. 'No news,' he heard from this station; 'no news' from that. He knew that he could not make himself heard, and even if he could have done he could have given them no favourable report. Night had fallen now; the wind had risen and so had the sea. The *America* was gradually losing height and dropping closer and closer to the heavy seas below. The men were tired, but no one could sleep—there was too great a chance of waking up in the Atlantic! During the night very little was said; a necessary word here and there; no more. The throbbing of their one engine was the only sound on board—and sometimes even this was almost drowned by the howling of the wind.

Wellman knew by this time that his dream of reaching Europe was over. They would be lucky now if they could get back to America safely. And without saying a word the others knew it too. Wellman looked at the massive eight-cylinder engine that had let them down so badly, and then at his silent companions, at the black sky, and at the heavy seas with their white horses threshing away below.

The obvious thing to do would have been to turn the helm towards the shore and make for home, but the situation was not so simple as that. The wind force was already so great that their one engine could no longer make any headway against it, and that cursed guide-rope which had seemed such a good idea was getting heavier and heavier, dragging the *America* lower and lower, swinging from left to right, threatening to stave in the lifeboat on which all their hopes of safety might soon depend, and causing the airship to heel over badly for minutes at a time, before painfully recovering.

Wellman realized that he could not put about if he wanted to. His airship was already practically a drifting hulk.

'We're between the devil and the deep blue sea, Vaniman,' he said frankly. 'We're sinking gradually lower and lower, and that can end only one way. And we're drifting, and that will take us away from the shipping routes and all hope of aid. We must lighten the ship, gain altitude and try to make the Bermudas or the coast of Florida, since the wind is now driving us south-eastward.'

'And how are we going to lighten her?' demanded Vaniman. 'We can't very well sacrifice our food supplies; we may have to stay in the air for another few days at least. There's the lifeboat, of course . . .'

'Out of the question,' interrupted Wellman. 'We may need it. You'll just have to get rid of all fuel-oil in excess of what you calculate will be necessary to take us to the Bermudas or the coast of Florida. That's our only chance. If we can lighten her she'll rise and be easier to manage. And for another thing, you can dismantle the eight-cylinder engine and pitch the pieces overboard.'

The first pools of oil began to appear below the airship, and as the eight-cylinder engine was dismantled, so piece after piece splashed into the sea. At midday Wellman succeeded in taking his bearings. The *America* was four hundred miles off the coast, and she was doing between fifteen and eighteen knots an hour. Thanks to the wind direction there was a good chance of reaching the Bermudas.

Hope of doing what they had originally set out to do had, of course, long vanished—and even the hope of getting back at all had fallen to a very low ebb. Now it rose again. Wellman was already thinking of 'next time' . . . But Irwin, the wireless operator interrupted with bad news.

'I've just received new signals; weak, but clear enough. There's a cyclone heading our way. It should catch up with us within the next forty-eight hours. We're advised to change course to avoid it.'

Change course? Wellman studied his maps. That was easier said than done. Even if they could maintain their present speed —which was far from certain—they would hardly be able to avoid it.

'What about launching our lifeboat right now?' suggested Vaniman.

'Too risky out of sight of a ship,' said Wellman. 'And in any case, we'd be safer on board here in the centre of a cyclone than in a small boat on the sea. No, our only chance is to fall in with a ship.'

'We've already been driven off the main transatlantic shipping routes,' said Vaniman, 'Still, we might be lucky . . .'

'There are plenty of tramp steamers and so on, apart from the main shipping lanes.'

Irwin spoke again. 'There's a chance here,' he said. 'A ship, the *Trent*, is leaving the Bermudas on Monday. Here's her course, and she's doing about twelve knots. At that rate we should converge next Thursday. If we can hold out that long and get that far we ought to have a chance.'

'Hold out' meant that the *America* must stay in the air and maintain her present speed—and that the cyclone mustn't catch up with her beforehand. The slow-moving *Trent* was, in fact, racing the cyclone for the lives of Wellman and his companions.

On Wednesday things were still going fairly well, but there were long silences in the gondola and nerves were obviously taut. The men walked around without any particular object in view, ate mechanically, and stroked the cat excessively. But the one thing they all did, half surreptitiously, was to keep a good look-out for the *Trent*. When night fell there was still no sign of her. Fortunately the weather had much improved, and a bright moon shone in a cloudless sky, making it possible to maintain the look-out.

Suddenly Wellman uttered an exclamation. South-south-west he could distinctly see lights—lighted portholes.

'That must be the *Trent*,' he said, and six pairs of eyes stared down eagerly. But what they saw was not the lights of one vessel, but of several; the lights of a fleet of vessels reflected in the water all around. Irwin rushed back to his wireless and sent out the C.Q.D. call—Come Quickly, Danger! And in the meantime Wellman searched with his sea glasses to catch any Morse reply. But the fleet below them remained silent and gave no sign.

'Surely they can see us,' thought Wellman puzzled. 'We must show up very clearly in this moonlight.' And then suddenly he realized what had happened.

'Discontinue calling, Irwin,' he ordered, and his voice had changed.

Vaniman had been studying the supposed ships below them with a telescope; he lowered it now, and looked at Wellman. He had realized, too. That little fleet of rescue vessels was an optical illusion caused by the broken reflection of the moon-light in the waves.

In the meantime the *America* was still slowly losing height, and at midnight they jettisoned further fuel-oil. Past twelve o'clock. This day was to be the day of their delivery. But would it be? They hoped to spot the *Trent* now far more desperately than they had previously hoped to fly the Atlantic. But how much chance had they? They were at the mercy of a number of things entirely beyond their control. The *Trent* might be late; contrary winds might drive them off their course. . . .

At two o'clock in the morning three of them tried to get some sleep.

At three o'clock the one remaining engine began to miss, and Vaniman anxiously attended to it.

At four o'clock the orange disc of the moon dropped below the horizon. As yet there was no sign of the dawn.

At half-past four Wellman ordered the searchlight to be switched on, and the three men who had been sleeping fitfully sprang to their feet. And then they all saw, almost without belief this time, what they had been looking for. There, about two miles away still, were the lights of a ship. There was no doubt about it this time; there were the red and the green navigation lights, and there, as though to underline the reality was the string of yellow cabin lights. It was the *Trent*.

Irwin was at the wireless key now, sending out their message. At first there was no reply, but after a few anxious minutes it came: 'S.S. *Trent* calling. S.S. *Trent* calling. Are you in difficulties?'

On board the *America* they sighed with relief when Irwin told them with a beaming face what was coming through. But they were not out of the wood yet. First of all they had to launch their lifeboat safely.

Captain Down of the *Trent* suggested that Wellman should wait for daylight, but as Wellman was no longer in full control of the dirigible, which was drifting; this meant that the *Trent* had to steam in the drift direction. This she did for two hours, and when she finally came close Wellman opened the valves and released the gas, bringing the *America* down to within thirty feet or so of the sea. All of them took their places in the lifeboat, and when they were no more than a few feet above the surface of the sea Wellman ordered the release mechanism to be operated. This was done, and the lifeboat dropped flat on to the surface, sending up a torrent of spray. Relieved of the weight of the lifeboat and its six occupants, the *America*, its sagging envelope flapping wildly, rapidly gained height and was carried away by the wind, which was swiftly rising as the first breath of the coming cyclone swept up.

'After three hours manœuvring, greatly hampered by a high wind, we managed to take on board the full crew of the airship *America*, including the ship's cat, all safe and sound. The airship was abandoned by her crew at latitude 35° 45′ north, longitude 68° west.'

This message, sent out by the S.S. *Trent*, ended the story of the first attempt to cross the Atlantic Ocean by air. The inquest now opened up. Most people were in agreement that the attempt had been foolish, and that Wellman had achieved nothing. The *America* had flown about twelve hundred miles before being abandoned, but that was far from offering any hope that the Atlantic could really be flown.

But Wellman was not discouraged, and he insisted that the Atlantic could and would be flown. The *America* had been too small. What was needed was an airship five times the size and, say, over six hundred feet long. Such an airship would have proper cabins lit by electricity, provided with telephones, and comfortably furnished with proper beds; and for the entertainment of the passengers there would be music rooms, smoking rooms, a restaurant, a library, and so on. Such an airship would, even in unfavourable weather conditions, carry passengers across the Atlantic at least 25 per cent faster than the fastest liner.

Wellman's enthusiastic prophecies made people smile—but there were some nevertheless who thought that perhaps, some day . . .

2

Read, Alcock and Brown, and the R-34

ON May 13th, 1919, a steamer carrying back soldiers to New York from the war in Europe encountered a U.S. cruiser off Newfoundland. It was making eastward escorted by three destroyers. The returning soldiers lined the rails and cheered the sailors, for whom they felt a certain collegial sympathy— those sailors had to carry on with their duties, whilst the men waving to them were thankfully going home to enjoy the peace and comfort of civilian life again, with no more early morning parades . . .

A few hours later the returning soldiers were again lining the deck rails, this time to stare at six more destroyers whose course went across that of their own ship.

'Why don't they give those boys a rest?' asked one of the soldiers sympathetically. 'It's all over over there now.'

But obviously the navy was not being allowed to rest on its laurels, for in the night the steamer sighted the lights of another flotilla of naval vessels two miles to port.

'Well, it's only an armistice, of course,' said the same soldier thoughtfully. 'Peace hasn't actually been signed yet. And you never know with those Fritzes.'

But actually those naval units were being sent out for an entirely different and quite peaceful purpose. Five days previously the Navy Department had ordered out five cruisers and over sixty destroyers, and their commanders had received precise instructions to take up their positions at points fifty miles from each other along a line extending from off New-foundland to the Azores. During the night they were to keep their searchlights going and strengthen their look-outs.

It was the beginning of a campaign which was to last something like twenty years, the campaign to subdue the Atlantic, to emancipate man from its storms, and establish swift and rapid communications between the Old World and the New by air. The first attempt to fly across the Atlantic Ocean with heavier than air machines was about to be made.

At first sight perhaps such a project must have seemed impossible in those days, in view of the vast distances involved and the state of technical development in the air. The biggest and most dramatic challenge was, of course, the stretch from New York to Paris, but that was a distance of 3,600 miles, and for the moment at least it really was out of the question. The stretch from Newfoundland to Ireland was not so bad, 'only' about 2,000 miles, but even that was out of the question for the time being. An airman who dared it would be placing himself completely at the mercy of the slightest technical defect: an overheated engine, a choked carburettor, a fuel-pipe failure . . . And then he would go down into the water and his only hope would be the faint possibility that a ship might turn up before his plane sank away under him.

So for these and other reasons, the U.S. Navy Department had decided to go cautiously, and not to ask its flyers to make the crossing in one non-stop flight, but to cross by stages. The longest and most dangerous of these stages was that from Newfoundland to the Azores, and to give them the biggest possible chance of survival in the event of their having to come down in the sea after all, this big fleet of vessels had been told off to take up positions along the 2,000-mile route. They would blaze the trail, so to speak, and at the same time be on hand to offer immediate assistance in case of need.

The machines chosen for the flight were big hydroplanes— big for those days at least—with a wing span of over 120 feet, powered by four 400-h.p. engines giving them a cruising speed of about ninety-five miles an hour, and with tanks holding almost 2,000 gallons of fuel. They carried a crew of six and were equipped with wireless. Three machines were to take part in the flight: the NC-1, the NC-3, and the NC-4.

The first two stages of the flight, Rockaway to Halifax and Halifax to Newfoundland, were flown without incident, and at 22.11 hours on May 16th the three hydroplanes rose into the air from the surface of Trepassey Bay. Nine years after Wellman's first attempt to fly the Atlantic, the Americans were trying again—but with heavier-than-air machines this time. The undertaking had been planned with the utmost care and no pains had been spared to make it a success. The naval Curtiss planes being used were quite capable of covering the distances from Newfoundland to the Azores. So in the Navy Department at Washington they sat back with confidence and waited for the upshot. But it was a confidence not unmixed with apprehension, for they were well aware that this undertaking was the first step towards a new era of world communications, an era in which the aeroplane would abolish distance, flying the Atlantic perhaps in a single night, so that a man could have his breakfast in Paris one morning and dine in New York the same night—or the other way round.

And along the route the powerful searchlights of the U.S. naval units lining the route swept the sky to guide the first men to attempt to link up the Old World and the New in heavier-than-air machines.

Early in the morning on May 17th men were listening eagerly for the first sound of engines in the sky and, at Fayal, Horta, Ounta Delgada and San Miguel, men's eyes searched the sky for those three black dots that would tell them the American airmen were arriving. It would have been more appropriate if the sky had been clear and the sun shining on such a day, but unfortunately the weather was miserable, and visibility was poor because of a steady drizzle which rendered the sea horizon invisible.

Hope and fear alternated now. Certainly the distance was easily within the range of those planes, but bad weather was an incalculable factor; and despite all the precautions which had been taken, and despite the skill and experience of the crews, accidents could happen and things could go wrong. After all, modern ships well able to withstand storms had mysteriously disappeared without trace before now, and by comparison those hydroplanes were fragile constructions of wood and wire. Although they could float, there was little doubt as to their fate if they were forced to come down in a heavy sea—unless help came quickly.

By midday fear was beginning to undermine hope. At one o'clock listeners thought they heard the sound of plane engines, but after straining their ears desperately they had to admit they had been mistaken. Then fishermen coming in with their boats claimed to have seen lights out to sea—it didn't make much sense. In the meantime the weather was worsening. But at 13.25 hours precisely there was the sound of engines in the air, so clearly that there was no doubt about it. In fact within a few moments a big plane appeared through the mist and came down on the surface of the harbour.

Hurriedly binoculars studied the plane. Yes, it was a Curtiss, and the markings showed it to be the NC-4—the machine flown by Lieut.-Comdr. Read, the leader of the three planes. But what had happened to the other two? For a while there was great anxiety for the safety of their crews, but then it was learned that the NC-1 had been compelled to come down in the sea about 180 miles away from Fayal, and that its crew had been rescued by the British tramp steamer *Jonah*. Bad weather had forced down the NC-3 even earlier, and its crew had been picked up by one of the U.S. destroyers strung out along the route for the purpose.

So one machine out of three had arrived safely. In view of the tremendous preparations and the extraordinary precautions taken to ensure the success of the flight, the result could hardly be regarded as an unqualified success. And as for a non-stop flight, say from Newfoundland to Ireland . . . Who was likely to try that?

The answer to that question was provided within a matter

of hours. On May 18th, the day after Read's arrival at the Azores, a Sopwith biplane powered by a 375-h.p. engine took off from Newfoundland heading across the Atlantic to Ireland, piloted by the well-known English aviator Hawker and his co-pilot Mackenzie Grieve. They had four hundred gallons of fuel in their tanks, enough to keep them in the air for about twenty-four hours and give them a margin of about three hundred miles—in reasonable weather. The plane took off at 19.00 hours, dropped its under-carriage to save weight, rose to a height of eight thousand feet and disappeared over the Atlantic.

Hawker and Mackenzie Grieve were the first men to try that dash across the Atlantic, and for many years it was to remain rash, sometimes dramatic, occasionally glorious. For a good many years such desperate attempts were little more than folly, for the early machines with which they were tried were capable of flying the distance only if all went well—and so often it didn't.

Hawker and Mackenzie Grieve were due to arrive over Ireland in the evening of May 19th, twenty-four hours after they had set off; watchers there were searching the sky for the first aeroplane to make the direct crossing from the New World to the Old. Those waiting in London and other towns for the news began to cheer and throw up their hats when the first report came in. The daring airmen had succeeded! But that enthusiasm did not last long, and the report was soon denied. The Sopwith had not been sighted.

Hours passed, and darkness closed in. The following morning it was only too clear that the two airmen could not arrive now. They had sufficient fuel for twenty-four hours approximately, no more. And nothing had been heard of them for thirty-six hours . . . It began to look as though the two brave and daring men were the first victims of transatlantic flight.

Then the master of a coaster reported that he had seen a plane plunge into the sea about forty miles off the west coast of Ireland. Eight destroyers immediately dashed to the spot and searched the neighbourhood, but in vain. The following

day, May 21st, and the day after that, nothing was heard. On
May 23rd came a report from the S.S. *Faraday* that a red light
had been seen at surface level. Once again destroyers raced to
the spot, but could find nothing. The search was continued on
May 24th. Then on May 25th the Admiralty ordered the
destroyers back to port, coastguard stations were instructed to
discontinue questioning passing vessels, and the search was
abandoned. The two intrepid flyers were given up for lost.

As a matter of routine, the men of the coastguard station at
the Butt of Lewis in the Outer Hebrides had, of course,
received the general instructions, but they had not been much
concerned in the search, for the route to have been followed
by Hawker and Mackenzie Grieve was very much farther
south. But on May 25th in the early evening they sighted a
small cargo boat making its way in shore on the violet sea.
When it was no more than a mile away it signalled its identity:
the Danish cargo-boat *Mary*, bound from New Orleans to
Horsens. The coastguard semaphore acknowledged the
information, but the master of the Danish boat had more to say.

'Have an aeroplane and crew on board,' he signalled.
'Britishers named Hawker and Grieve.'

The coastguards stared at each other as the Morse signals
were received: so Hawker and Mackenzie Grieve were alive
after all! Instead of being the first victims of transatlantic
flight they were the first survivors.

The Admiralty were informed at once; the destroyer H.M.S.
Woolston put out at once to meet the *Mary*, and on May 27th
Hawker and Mackenzie Grieve arrived in London to be
greeted by crowds wild with enthusiasm.

There was something miraculous about their rescue. After
flying for something like four hours they encountered a strong
north wind, and rose to about fifteen thousand feet to get
above it, but then their engine was suddenly hidden in clouds
of steam, and Hawker realized that a cooling duct must be
blocked. It was impossible to remedy it in the air, so he
decided to fly southward towards the more frequented shipping

lanes, knowing that sooner or later he would have to go down. Three hours passed, and the engine was overheating badly. Things looked black, particularly as the weather was steadily worsening.

Anxiously the two men studied the sea in every direction. A ship was their only hope now, and both of them knew it. They also realized that if they spotted one just in the nick of time it would be little short of miraculous. But they were lucky. They spotted the S.S. *Mary*. That is to say, they spotted her smoke first, for it was being beaten down flat by the wind. But there she was, pitching and rolling in the heavy seas, ploughing her way steadily through the spume and drift. Hawker spiralled down towards her, and the master of the Danish vessel was in no doubt as to what was required of him. Almost before the plane hit the sea a boat was lowered.

Thankfully Hawker and his companion clambered on board and shook hands with the Danish skipper and his men. Then Hawker asked the worthy Captain to let London know what had happened. Of course, they were not yet overdue, but their relatives and friends would want to know that though they had failed they were safe at least.

'I can't do that,' said the Captain. 'The *Mary* hasn't any wireless.'

And the *Mary* hadn't any speed either, so it took them six days to reach the Butt of Lewis and signal the news to the coastguard station there. The captain might have put into an Irish port rather earlier, but as the two airmen were safe and in the best of health he didn't feel justified in changing course, particularly as he hoped to meet some other vessel on the way —perhaps one with wireless. But as luck would have it not another vessel of any kind was sighted. It was as though the little *Mary* were alone on the high seas. But then at last, on May 25th, the incredible news was flashed around the world. Hawker and Mackenzie Grieve, who had been given up for lost, were safe after all!

People recalled that traditionally fortune favoured the brave, and those other airmen nursing plans of their own were strengthened in their resolves. A flyer named Raynham was the next to try. He took off from Newfoundland, but crashed before he was over the sea. Help was rushed to the spot at once. Not only was he alive, but unhurt. The luck of the Atlantic flyers was holding!

And now the French joined in. Roget and Coli announced their intention of attempting a non-stop crossing Paris to New York—at a time when the range of most machines was hardly three thousand miles! Folly? Yes, but it was a kind of mass folly which had seized on flyers and made even the most cautious optimistic. After all, no one had given Christopher Columbus a dog's chance. You just had to try. Daring and courage could win through where caution must fail. And then to add a little material encouragement an American of French extraction, Raymond Orteig, offered a prize of 25,000 dollars for the first airman or airmen to cross the Atlantic in a non-stop flight from New York to Paris or vice-versa. Obviously Read's non-stop flight from Newfoundland to the Azores was just a beginning, a mere forerunner of the much longer flights that would now be attempted—and performed.

The immediate stage was the 2,000-mile jump from New-foundland to Ireland, the jump that had beaten Hawker and Mackenzie Grieve. Two men came forward as the next candidates. Both were British; they were ex-officers of the war which was just over, Captain John Alcock and Lieutenant Arthur W. Brown, using a converted Vickers-Vimy bomber powered by two Rolls-Royce engines of 350 h.p. giving it a cruising speed of 90 miles per hour. They made careful preparations and then waited for favourable weather, and on June 14th came the news that they had started at 16.28 hours from Newfoundland and were on their way to Ireland.

Expectantly the world now awaited their signals, for this time the transatlantic flyers had wireless. But no messages were received. The next day, June 15th, planes were sent out along the route the Vickers-Vimy was to follow. Alcock and

Brown were to be escorted in—if they could be found, for it was not at all sure where they would try to land; so much would depend on the weather, and the weather was no longer good. There was thick mist and a strong wind, but at least it was a tailwind for them. All the airfields which came into question were warned to be on the look-out.

At 08.30 hours the sound of an engine was heard in the air over Clifden aerodrome; a plane came in to land, rolled along uncertainly and then stood on its nose. Two men crawled out of its cockpit and introduced themselves to the airfield personnel who came running up.

'Alcock and Brown.'

At the news of their safe arrival a wave of relief and enthusiasm swept the British Isles, and it was all the more tremendous because their wireless silence on the way had given rise to secret fears for their safety. Apparently the crossing had not been easy.

'It was pretty chancy,' said Alcock. 'Once or twice, in fact, we thought our number was up.'

Immediately after the take-off in the late afternoon, the heavily loaded machine had put the hearts of the watchers into their mouths by almost crashing into the side of a hill, but it had managed to rise above it, and, accompanied by the blaring of ships' sirens in St. John's Bay it had disappeared over the Atlantic in an easterly direction.

The first thing that went wrong was the wireless, and when Brown tried to send out the first signal he found that the generator was out of order. He did his best to repair it, but it was hopeless. That was a pity; first of all it meant that they could give out no information about their progress, and secondly, which was very much worse, they would be unable to ask for information as to their position from ships in the neighbourhood. They could still receive messages, however, and they could hear ships down below talking about them and asking for news. But they were unable to give any.

The second spot of trouble occurred when they were about

three hundred miles out from Newfoundland—and it was worse than the first. Flames began to shoot out of their exhaust, and it was soon glowing red. Brown spotted it first, and for a while they thought they were on fire, but then they realized that it wasn't so bad. Should they go on, or try to get back to Newfoundland?

'Let's go on,' said Alcock, and Brown agreed.

In the end the exhaust broke away and fell into the sea. Fortunately the two engines were still running quite smoothly.

When night fell, however, there was more trouble. They had chosen a night when the moon should have been shining brightly—and no doubt it was so doing somewhere far up above those clouds. But that didn't help them down below, and they had to go down low and fly just above the waves.

It was very cold, too. Despite the low altitude ice began to form on the wings, and the Vickers-Vimy grew heavier, slower and less manageable. But towards morning the temperature rose, the ice melted, and ran off the plane as water, and once again the machine answered readily to the controls. When daylight came it was not long before they saw land on the horizon—Ireland, the first outpost of Europe in the North Atlantic.

In London they were given a triumphant reception, together with Hawker and Mackenzie Grieve. Alcock and Brown had done it. They were the first men to fly the Atlantic in non-stop flight, and it was to be a good many years before it was done again; so long, in fact, that the world was inclined to forget that it had ever been done at all. But even as they responded to the ovations of the crowd they knew that their success was not due altogether to the qualities of their machine or even to their own flying and navigational skill. Aeroplanes were still not good enough to conquer the Atlantic as a matter of course. You needed luck as well, and they had had it. If the wind had not been in their favour, if the mist had not dispersed, if . . . And they might not have sighted a ship at the crucial moment as their colleagues Hawker and Mackenzie Grieve had done.

No, their triumph had been due largely to luck. To fly across the Atlantic regularly and safely, bigger and more powerful planes would be necessary. How long would it be before the aero industry could provide them?

Wellman had not succeeded in his attempt, but there were some people who thought that he had nevertheless had the right idea—transatlantic crossing by airship. At least an airship didn't have to come down in the sea if its engines happened to fail. 'But they're too slow,' argued the supporters of the heavier-than-air machines. 'They're too fragile, too much at the mercy of wind and weather if their engines should fail; and even more subject to icing than planes.'

But it was a fact that the German airships, the Zeppelins, could fly—theoretically at least—five or six thousand miles non-stop, which would be quite enough to cross the Atlantic. One man, the Comte de La Vaulx, showed a lively awareness of their possibilities, because in an article in the *Matin* he demanded that the peace treaty, which had not yet been signed at Versailles, should contain a clause confiscating all Germany's Zeppelins to prevent their establishing a monopoly of transatlantic flight.

There were experts in Great Britain who were far from despising the airship; in fact two big airships—the R-33 and the R-34—were already being prepared for long-distance flights, and there was even talk of their being used for an Atlantic crossing. 'It won't be long now,' said those in the know, and they were right.

On July 2nd at 02.18 hours, when the first faint signs of dawn were in the sky, an airship rose slowly into the sky from the airfield at East Fortune on the first attempt to fly the Atlantic in the east–west direction. It was the R-34, under the command of Major G. G. Scott, 660 feet long, with a capacity of 1,940,000 cubic feet and powered by five Sunbeam engines each of 270 h.p., giving her a cruising speed of rather less than 50 miles per hour.

Theoretically the R-34 had a range of about four thousand

miles, quite enough to allow her to fly across the Atlantic, but
her commander knew that other factors were involved: contrary winds and bad weather, including mist and fog. The
weather difficulties might well be considerable, because the
date of the flight had been fixed arbitrarily long in advance of
any possibility of accurate weather forecasts, precisely in order
to make the experiences on the flight more convincing and
conclusive.

The first trouble they had to face was a heavy mist. The R-34
was already over the Atlantic. Scott was not disturbed, and he
could see that his men were not either, though the mist was
soon so thick as almost to muffle the sound of their engines.
An airship was not at the mercy of an engine failure, and it
could float quite safely without power. Moreover its crew
lived in relatively comfortable conditions. They could talk
easily, move around freely, and, in fact, behave more or less
as though they were on the ground. Some of them were
leaning against the deck rail as though they were on an ocean
liner. 'And that's in fact what we are,' thought Scott—'the
ocean-going liners of the future will be airships.'

He walked along to the wireless cabin.

'Anything from the *Tiger* or the *Renown*?' he asked.

'No, sir.'

The *Renown* and the *Tiger* were warships steaming along the
line of flight to keep in wireless touch with the R-34, and to
be on hand to give any assistance that might be needed.

The mist persisted, but from time to time it parted enough
to allow the sun to shine through and to reveal the wide
expanse of green sea below. Then it would close in once more,
and the R-34 would again be surrounded by a cloud of grey
cotton wool.

A hot meal was served as usual at midday; there was no need
for thermos flasks and hastily swallowed sandwiches on this
Atlantic trip. Afterwards, those of the men who were not on
duty followed their own devices. Some of them took an afternoon snooze in their hammocks; but they hadn't been down

long before they were startled to hear the sound of their commander's voice angrily giving someone a thorough dressing-down. They could hear him even above the noise of the engines and the whistling of the wind through the cordage.

They found out afterwards that the master-at-arms had brought him a stowaway who had been found on board, a young fellow of twenty, who had not been mustered as one of the crew, but who was determined not to be left out. He stood there before the commander, standing to attention and letting the Major's anger descend on him.

'Do you know what you've done, you young fool?' the Major demanded. 'By stowing yourself away you have compromised our success. The weight has been calculated down to the last pound. If I did my plain duty I'd have you pitched overboard. Your presence will reduce our range by many miles.'

The annoyed major was exaggerating. The young fellow's weight would have made all the difference in the world to an aeroplane—in fact, just such a stowaway spoiled one transatlantic flight—but it really didn't make a great deal of difference to the R-34. Still, there must be discipline . . .

The R-34 continued on her way, but not so fast as had been hoped because she now had to contend with headwinds which slowed her down. From time to time she nosed her way through thick clouds, but she was keeping her course well.

At about 19.00 hours the W/T operator informed the commander that he was receiving Newfoundland. That was a foretaste of success, though three-quarters of the journey still remained to be flown.

'Anything from the *Renown*?'

'Yes, sir. We're in touch now. They're checking our course.'

That check was very necessary, because the R-34 was flying practically blind the whole time. The mist was so heavy that twilight fell unnoticed, and a steady downpour began to beat on the envelope of the dirigible. By morning, when the weather was no better, the R-34 was flying over the area where Hawker and Mackenzie Grieve had been picked up. Looking down into the grey sea stretching away endlessly below it was not difficult to realize that their rescue had been little short of miraculous.

'It's safer up here,' observed one of the officers. And he was right, particularly as so far the R-34 had been in luck. It was true that she was not making the progress which had been expected of her, but at least she was going forward steadily, and, so far at least, their engines had not given them the slightest trouble. But as so often, as soon they began to con-gratulate themselves on their good fortune, something went wrong. The noise of the engines was no longer so steady, and from time to time there were even small explosions. One of the starboard engines was giving trouble.

'A piston, sir,' reported one of the engineers.

'Can you repair it?'

'Temporarily; enough to get us to New York, I hope.'

The engineer was as good as his word, and within a couple of hours all five engines were running smoothly again. The delay caused was negligible—as far as that minor breakdown was concerned. But the delay being caused by the adverse weather conditions was another matter. The wind was very high now, and there were rain squalls so violent that the helmsman had difficulty in keeping the R-34 on course.

Scott decided to go up higher, but at 2,300 feet there was no change, and when he went still higher the rolling and pitching seemed if anything to get worse. Finally, at well over three thousand feet, conditions were rather better. During the night they improved still further, and the R-34 was able to go forward steadily under a starlit sky.

Scott went to the wireless cabin. 'What's the weather forecast?' he asked.

'Not particularly hopeful, sir. Thick fog reported from Newfoundland.'

That was certainly not particularly hopeful. Over the sea the mist did not really bother the R-34 much, but for landing a certain visibility was essential.

The following morning the mist lifted from time to time and large stretches of green sea became visible below. Icebergs were floating menacingly in the water. They had sunk more than one great vessel in the past. 'At least they're no danger to us,' thought Scott.

Everyone on board was keyed up now, and the men were keeping a sharp look-out ahead in the hope of seeing the thin dark line on the horizon. 'Not a hope before the afternoon,' said an officer. But the men still kept their look-out. 'Like Christopher Columbus's sailors,' joked the officer.

And he wasn't so far out, because this was certainly the first time that anyone would sight the New World from the air, and the men were anxious to be the first.

At 13.00 hours there was a light mist, but it was heavy enough to cloud the horizon and make it impossible to distinguish land except at very close range. However, Scott noted with satisfaction that the wind was rising. Perhaps it would drive away the mist. And, in fact, it did.

At about half-past one a shout went up, followed by another and then another. Land had been sighted.

'Newfoundland,' said Scott quietly. He did his best not to betray the excitement that was rising in him. They had done it. The first east–west crossing of the Atlantic by air had been accomplished.

He glanced at the chronometer in its case: 13.50 hours; it had taken them 59 hours to fly from East Fortune to their first sight of the New World. He made a swift calculation: 2,360 miles in 59 hours; that was an average speed of 40 miles per hour, which wasn't very fast going. However, speed wasn't everything. The great thing was that it had been done, and done against adverse winds and in unfavourable weather. It was this which justified the hope that before long it would be possible to establish regular airship services over the Atlantic.

Everyone on board was in high spirits now—even the

stowaway, who had a court-martial to look forward to when they returned. Eagerly they studied every detail of Trinity Bay as they flew over it. Its shores looked bleak and desolate, but at least there was a little sunshine to brighten up their first glimpse of the New World.

Scott was in the chart room poring over his maps. His journey was not over yet. There was another thousand miles or so to go, but at least the Atlantic crossing was behind them. They would no longer be alone over the sea, but in constant touch with U.S. wireless stations, and help would be readily available if necessary. He was therefore not greatly disturbed when at about five o'clock that afternoon the mist and fog closed in on the R-34 again. When night fell and the grey mass all around became black he had every reason to hope that it would lighten by daybreak, for the weather stations told him that a fresh breeze was blowing along the coasts of Nova Scotia ahead of him. But when he asked the wind direction they told him that it was preponderantly westward, which was bad. It meant headwinds and a consequent reduction of speed.

As daybreak approached the weather worsened, and Scott began to feel anxious. He was going forward into the heart of a low pressure area with heavy storms. A tremendous amount of interference was crackling and spluttering in the ear-phones of his W/O and spoiling reception, while all around were the blue flashes of electrical storms in the sky. The engines were still running smoothly, but the headwinds were so strong that the R-34 was hardly making any progress at all. Scott found it difficult to believe that the engines were giving their full power, but his engineer assured him that they were.

'How much fuel-oil have we left?' he demanded.

'Enough for rather more than twenty-four hours, sir.'

Theoretically this was an amply sufficient margin, but practically . . . The R-34 was doing little more than maintain her position, and it was as much as she could do to keep her head into the wind. Scott considered his situation. To use his remaining fuel merely marking time would not do, but if he tried to tack, as sailing ships did, the great bulk of the dirigible would offer a greater purchase to the wind, and then it would be impossible to prevent her being driven off course. In other words, there was no easy solution. They would just have to keep on course as far as possible, and hope for the best. There was general apprehension on board now. From time to time they could see the waves below them through breaks in the cloud. It was a heavy sea, constantly thrashed by violent squalls, and each time they could see the waves more clearly. They were losing height.

'We're losing gas, sir,' reported an officer.

'Try to gain altitude, though,' ordered Scott. 'At this height a sudden heavy squall might force us down into the sea.'

'Very good, sir.'

The R-34 started to rise, but with difficulty. Then suddenly there was a jolt and the men had to grab at the nearest thing to hand to keep their feet; one or two of them actually fell and rolled along the wet deck. The R-34 had been caught in a giant whirlwind, and she reared upwards—500 feet, 650 feet, 800 feet. The officers watched the sudden ascent anxiously; they knew that it might end in an equally sudden descent, and that might end in the sea. The roaring of the wind was louder than the noise of the five engines now, and indeed the engines sounded like a faint moan in the background. All the men were clinging on to some hold and waiting for the downward lurch.

When it came it felt as though the deck of the R-34 were sinking away beneath their feet. Scott stared at the dial of the altimeter. The descent was even more rapid than the ascent had been.

'Two thousand feet,' he said as he caught one of his officers looking at him inquiringly. 'No danger of hitting the sea at the moment.'

'At the moment.' But what about the situation in an hour or two if the loss of gas continued? Scott was well aware of the danger.

'Alter course to the south-west,' he ordered.

He knew that to scud before the wind meant to avoid any immediate risk of shipwreck, but it also meant to increase the risk of being blown out to sea without fuel. In the meantime the consumption was disquieting, particularly as there was no telling how long they would have to remain in the air. America and safety had been close ahead, but suddenly a great wall of wind had risen to head them off, and now they were being compelled to skirt that wall. Sometimes they plunged down towards the crests of those prancing white horses below, sometimes they shot up; and now and again their irregular dash seem to halt altogether as though the engines had stopped.

Scott was in the navigation cabin the whole time. His original aim had been to reach New York, but now his main aim was to save his ship even if he had to abandon his objective. It was no dishonour for a ship to break off her voyage and seek shelter from heavy storms in a neighbouring port. For him that meant a mooring mast, either on land or at sea. A ship could take him in tow and, if need be, save his crew. He called the W/O.

'Are you still in touch with land stations?' he asked.

'With some difficulty, sir, yes. The aerial keeps breaking and has to be repaired. Both transmission and reception are being distorted by the storm, but I *am* still in contact.'

'Very good. Then tell New York our position and repeat it every quarter of an hour. Explain that we're in difficulties, and ask if they can send out destroyers to help us; perhaps to take us in tow.'

'Very good, sir.'

But it was no easy matter to fix a rendezvous with a ship at sea; the R-34 was unable to stay put and wait, and her progress was so irregular that it was very difficult to say with any accuracy where she was likely to be in a few hours' time, and what now began was an involuntary game of hide and seek.

Fortunately there was a squadron of destroyers lying in Boston harbour with steam up, and they were able to put to sea at once. The white foam raced away from their stems, waves swept over their decks and spray lashed the glass of their bridge housing as they turned out to sea to the assistance of the R-34. Their course was very much of a guess, but they hoped to be able to correct it from time to time as they received news from the dirigible.

'Make towards the Bay of Fundy,' Scott had said, though he had realized perfectly well that he might not be able to reach it. In fact the wind actually drove him over Cape Sable. Towards evening he ordered a W/T message to be sent out: 'Have fuel for twelve hours only.'

Night fell on the last stage of the adventure. The U.S. destroyers reached the Bay of Fundy and studied the sky in vain for any sight or sound of the R-34. Their searchlights showed them only low-lying clouds racing across the sky, clouds which diffused the beams of their searchlights and lit up the sea rather than the sky. From time to time a destroyer's gun barked—blank shot fired in the hope of attracting the attention of the R-34 and producing some reply; perhaps a coloured rocket from the gondola. But there was silence in the skies, broken only by the howling of the wind and the crashing of heavy seas.

No further wireless signals were being received from the R-34, and the searchers began to wonder whether the silence was because she had already been forced down into the sea.

For two days everything had been ready for mooring the R-34 on Mineola airfield in New York State, but the ground personnel there was still waiting. On the morning of July 6th the sky was still so heavy with storm clouds that it wasn't easy to tell that the sun had risen at all—the only really reliable evidence was the clock. The men were still in a state of alert, but it didn't look as though they would be called upon this day any more than on the others. Within a few hours the R-34 would be without fuel; and, in any case, nothing had been heard of her since the previous evening.

But at eight-thirty that morning news was reported. People on Long Island declared that they had seen the cigar-like shape of an airship through the clouds for a moment or two. It wasn't taken very seriously, and it hadn't been the first false report. The arrival of the R-34 had even been announced. But the mooring mast was still empty . . .

The officers and men at Mineola were silent and depressed. They could imagine only too well the last desperate struggles of their British comrades; the airship drifting helplessly, its silk sides flapping for want of gas, one engine after the other stopping for want of fuel, the propellors spinning more and more slowly and then stopping for good; the last frantic efforts to gain altitude, and finally the crash as the gondolas hit the waves; the sagging mass of the envelope as it sprawled across the sea; and then the end . . . Perhaps it was happening at this very moment?

'And they came so near doing it,' sighed one of the airfield officers regretfully. 'It was a bit too soon. At least they should have chosen their weather. There wasn't all that hurry.'

And then there was a sudden shout. All eyes went to the sky. Orders were bawled, and men began to run towards the mast. A great airship had suddenly appeared through the clouds, her engines still running as she circled round the airfield. It was the R-34; there was no doubt about it. Scott and his men had done it after all. There were the identification markings in huge black letters across the envelope—'R-34'.

But for the moment the airship circled over the field and seemed to be waiting for something. All eyes were staring up at her when suddenly there was a shout of alarm as they saw a man jump from the gondola; as he hurtled down there was horrified silence. Then a parachute opened out behind him and broke his fall, causing him to sail down gently to land a little distance away. He was already getting out of his harness when they ran up to him.

'Major Pritchard,' he said introducing himself.

'Glad to meet you, sir,' said an American officer shaking his hand. 'You sure did give us a fright, though. Anything wrong up there?'

'No, nothing at all. I've just come down to advise on mooring operations.'

Four days later, at midnight, the R-34 cast off from the mooring mast at Mineola and started her homeward journey.

'Naturally we won't have finished the job until we're safely home again,' said Scott to journalists. 'As you know, we had our difficulties on the way here, but I'm more convinced than ever that airships will be able to establish a regular transatlantic service, and I'm anxious to prove it.'

It had taken the R-34 108 hours to reach America, but assisted by favourable winds, she made the return journey without incident in 73 hours. On July 13th at 07.00 hours she was moored safely to the great mast at Pulham airfield in Norfolk.

The outward and homeward voyage of the R-34 across the Atlantic, only nine years after Wellman's first attempt, certainly lent colour to Scott's contention that, in the existing state of aeronautical technique at least, the airship was the most suitable means for flying the Atlantic—'in safety and comfort', as its supporters declared.

'But only slowly,' objected those who still favoured heavier-than-air machines. 'After all, the *Lusitania* made the crossing from Liverpool to New York in 106 hours in 1909— and in even greater safety and comfort. So what's the point of going by airship? No, the only advantage of flying the Atlantic will lie in being able to do it much more quickly.'

To which the airship supporters replied: 'It's true that the R-34 took 108 hours to do the crossing, but she happened to meet with exceptionally unfavourable conditions. Normally speaking she would do it much more quickly—and she's never likely to take longer.'

Neither party succeeded in convincing the other, and the

debate was to go on for a long time, with each side putting forward its arguments again and again. The aeroplane meant greater speed, certainly, but airship meant greater safety and comfort. Take your choice.

There was another card in the heavier-than-air pack: the hydroplane or flying boat, which could come down on the sea safely in the event of engine trouble: 'as two of Read's hydroplanes did, for example.'

Unfortunately there was one man who was unable to take part in these lively discussions, and that was the pioneer aeronaut Wellman. He had not lived to see the airship cross and re-cross the Atlantic in triumph as he had said it would eventually do. He had been killed in an accident in 1912.

3

The Battle for the South Atlantic

ON January 22nd, 1926, at eight o'clock in the morning a
two-engined hydroplane flew low round the statue of
Christopher Columbus at Palos de Moguer—the port from
which the famous navigator put out on his voyage to the New
World—and flew away on a southward course. It was the
preliminary homage paid to the discoverer of America by
Commander Franco before setting off in his hydroplane the
Plus Ultra on a flight from Spain to Brazil and on to the
Argentine.

Two Portuguese flyers, Captain Sacadura Cabral and
Captain Giago Coutinho, had already flown across the South
Atlantic from Portugal to Brazil, but it had taken them two
months and three different machines before they managed to
reach Rio de Janeiro. They had taken off from Lisbon on
March 30th, 1922, to do the journey in stages: to the Canaries,
from there to the Cape Verde Islands, and on to St. Paul
Rocks, where they had crashed, about 375 miles from the
coast of Brazil. A new plane had been sent to them, but had
broken down at the island of Fernando Noronha. Whilst in
tow to the Portuguese cruiser *Republica* the machine had been
damaged so badly that a third plane had had to be sent, and it
was in this that the two flyers, who had been dogged by bad
luck, finally completed their flight.

This qualified success left the field open, and Commander
Franco now set off in his hydroplane with three companions,
seeking, above all, to bring the time for the crossing down to
reasonable proportions. Once again the flight was to be made

in stages: the Canaries, the Cape Verde Islands, Pernambuco, Rio de Janeiro, and finally Buenos Aires.

On January 22nd at 16.00 hours Franco's plane came down on the surface of the sea at Las Palmas in the Canaries—and it was high time. They had had considerable difficulty in finding their way. Franco and his companions stayed a few days in Las Palmas, overhauling their engines and hoping for better weather. Then on January 26th they took off again, making for the Cape Verde Islands, their next objective.

'I reckon to touch down at Porto Praya before nightfall,' Franco had said.

Porto Praya was the main harbour of San Iago, one of the Cape Verde Islands, and the distance was about eleven hundred miles. At 12.45 hours the steamer *San Carlos* sighted the hydroplane and got in touch by wireless. Franco reported that all was well. Three hours later another message was received by the wireless station at Porto Piezzo: his average speed was about 90 miles per hour. All was well, and there was nothing further to report. This time Franco was favoured by the weather, and he arrived at Porto Praya at 20.00 hours the same evening as planned.

The meteorological reports were favourable, and the north-west trade winds were blowing. Franco thereupon decided to leave at dawn the next day. He even considered making the hop from the Cape Verde Islands to Brazil non-stop, but he finally decided that night moorings at Pernambuco would be dangerous. The two normal stages were St. Paul Rocks and Fernando Noronha, but he decided to use one of them only. In fact he regarded these two islands less as stages than as havens in the event of trouble. However, he asked by wireless that the port authorities at both these places should make ready to receive him.

At dawn the next morning the four men were taken out to their hydroplane, a big machine with a low hull surmounted by two 500 h.p. engines in tandem. The sea was calm and there was a light breeze. The *Plus Ultra* took off smoothly and disappeared southward. Two hours later the sea began to rise under the steady blowing of the trade wind.

'If I had to go down now we'd be in a bit of a jam,' thought Franco. But fortunately his engines were running smoothly, and there was really nothing to justify any apprehension. The wind was behind them, and it not only helped them on but did something to temper the heat in the cabin, which by this time was getting so torrid that occasionally it made them gasp for breath.

Despite his sudden thought, Franco was quite confident that he was going to succeed. He would have been very much astonished to learn that at that very moment people were worrying about him and his crew, and that there were even rumours that his machine had been lost. It was 19.00 hours, and for some time they had been on the look-out for him at St. Paul Rocks, but without result, and as no wireless messages had been picked up the authorities were beginning to fear the worst.

'Franco left this morning,' flashed San Iago at the Cape Verde Islands to St. Paul.

'In that case he ought to be here by now,' replied St. Paul. 'It's beginning to look as though he may have had to go down in the sea. If that's so there's no means of looking for him.'

But St. Paul was too pessimistic; Franco and his companions were still safely airborne in the *Plus Ultra*, and rapidly approaching Fernando Noronha.

'Are we going to put down at Noronha?' inquired Ruiz de Alda.

Franco considered for a while. The place was not well suited for hydroplanes, and there was no good harbour where they could put down safely. In addition there was a dangerous on-shore swell, and there would be a good deal of risk to their hull in putting down on it.

'It might be as well to fly straight on to Pernambuco,' commented Ruiz de Alda.

'How much fuel have we got left, Prata?' asked Franco.

'A couple of hundred gallons.'

That was enough to get them to Brazil, but to put down on the sea at Pernambuco at night would be no small risk either.

'There *is* Fernando Noronha,' interjected Ruiz de Alda.

The sombre island grew larger in the failing daylight, and Franco went down and made a reconnaissance sweep over the surface of the sea. It was as he had feared: the sea was high, choppy and very unfavourable for setting the hydroplane down. He regained height, and considered the situation. It was rapidly getting darker now, and he would have to make up his mind quickly: on the one hand there was the increasing dark-ness—a risk in itself—and on the other there was the choppy sea. Whatever he did there would be a risk in it. He decided to touch down.

Carefully he chose the spot where he thought he could do so with the least risk, and then, with a grave, set face, he gently turned down the nose of the hydroplane so that the descent towards the sea was gradual. After a while spray began to beat against the windows, and then the noise of the waves mingled with the roar of the engines. Suddenly there was a bump, and then another one until the whole hull was being shaken violently. Entering the water the port float dug itself into the waves. Franco immediately pulled the machine round, but they pitched heavily; a fountain of water and spray rose into the air, and as the nose of the hydroplane dipped, one of the propellers hit the surface. Prata immediately switched off the engine, but it was too late: a propeller blade had been damaged.

With his one remaining engine Franco turned the hydro-plane shorewards, coming nearer the coast, but not approach-ing too closely for fear they might be dashed against the rocks and destroyed. He was already regretting the decision he had taken, but it was quite impossible to change it now; to take off again for Pernambuco with only one engine was out of the question. He had the hydroplane's head into the waves, and was considering dropping a drag anchor in the hope of main-taining his position until morning, when on shore they noticed a large group of men in striped costume obviously trying to launch a raft.

'They're convicts!' exclaimed Ruiz de Alda.

He was right, and as they looked more closely they could see warders too. They were clearly attempting to come to the assistance of the hydroplane. The raft was a good idea. There would be less danger for the hydroplane with a raft than the off-shore rocks, but first of all the raft would have to be got out to sea and anchored securely. As it was, an on-shore wind and the swell were making it very difficult to get the raft away from the shore at all. The convicts were doing their best; some of them were up to their necks in the water whilst others were actually swimming and dragging on stout hawsers.

'They're not going to manage it,' muttered Franco. Only too well he realized that you could plan a flight like this as carefully as you liked, and you would always be at the mercy of some unforeseen difficulty.

But fortunately as night fell so did the wind, and the convicts did finally succeed in getting the raft out to sea and anchoring it securely, after which, the *Plus Ultra* experienced very little difficulty in manœuvring alongside and making fast.

'I think I'll stay on board for the night,' said Franco. In his mind he could imagine the ridiculous situation of a pilot without a plane. If somehow in the night the hydroplane broke loose and drifted away he would find himself staring out to sea in the morning—a laughing-stock.

'No,' said de Alda firmly. 'You've been piloting her all day long. You must get some proper sleep. Prata, Druan and I will stay on board.'

At first Franco refused to agree, but in the end he allowed himself to be persuaded, and he went ashore to spend a few hours in fitful sleep. Shortly after dawn he hurried down to the shore. The *Plus Ultra* was safe, and mechanics were already repairing the damage to the propeller, which was soon in a fit state to take them on to Pernambuco. There had been no damage to the hull, but the sea was so choppy that a take-off would clearly be very difficult, so they spent the morning overhauling the engines.

In the afternoon, at 15.00 hours, Franco made a first attempt to get away, watched with interest by the convicts, who had probably saved them the evening before. He taxied along the surface for a few thousand yards and then returned to his original moorings. At the second attempt he succeeded in getting the hydroplane into the air.

'Do you think you could manage to get us to Pernambuco on one engine?' demanded Druan.

'I think so; why not?' asked Franco, adding: 'Two engines are essential only for the take-off.'

'Well, the forward engine is over-heating.'

'Very well,' said Franco, 'we'll use only the rear engine, then.'

For a while things went well, but at 18.00 hours the rear engine began to give signs of trouble, and they grew anxious.

'There's only one thing for it,' decided Franco: 'we must lighten the machine as far as possible. Jettison what petrol you can, and our water supply. If we have to go down in this we'll go under before help can reach us.'

An hour later they anxiously began to scan the horizon ahead for the saving coast line they knew could not be far off. Luck was on their side; at 19.15 hours they spotted a dark line on the horizon and they heaved sighs of relief. At 19.30 hours the *Plus Ultra* touched down on the sea off Pernambuco without further trouble, but with practically empty tanks.

For various reasons they had to extend their stay at Pernambuco for four days, but at last, at dawn on February 4th, they took off again. That evening they touched down safely at Rio de Janeiro, having flown over thirteen hundred miles in fifteen hours.

On February 9th, after trying for five hours to take off, and being delayed by a series of mishaps, Franco finally got the hydroplane into the air and set course for Montevideo. The next day he touched down safely at Buenos Aires to conclude a flight which had taken seventeen days in all.

Though it took almost three weeks, Franco's flight was the first decisive air victory over the South Atlantic, and the conquest was confirmed when the Italian General de Pinedo touched down with his hydroplane *Santa Maria* at Bahia on February 25th, 1927. However, this second flight had not gone altogether smoothly. The *Santa Maria* had developed engine trouble and had had to be assisted by a Brazilian cruiser, and during the towing operations the hydroplane had suffered damage.

Despite this the flight was a success, and it took de Pinedo and his crew to Buenos Aires and New York. Then, on June 16th, they went on to Rome in a second hydroplane identical with the first, which had been destroyed. But de Pinedo was anxious to do better and to make the flight without having recourse to any assistance from surface vessels, and without having to use more than one machine.

A few days after his arrival in Bahia, watchers at Casablanca were made curious by the presence of another hydroplane which had touched down there and seemed to have been abandoned. The press announced that the Uruguayan Commandant Glauco Larre Borges was about to attempt a transatlantic flight with a crew of three, including his brother Taddeo, and two other men named Ibarra and Rigoli. Details of their hydroplane were given. It had two engines of 500 h.p., a range of 2,500 miles, and it carried 920 gallons of petrol. It was to be guided on the way by the wireless of the S.S. *Mendoza*, on board which the commandant's wife and his four children would make the crossing.

But when the time came for the take-off, the hydroplane, the *Uruguay*, remained silently at its moorings. And the day after that, too . . . Then it was announced that the crew were engaged in a complete overhaul of its engines, which seemed strange. After all, only two stages of the journey had been flown so far; and when even this was no longer sufficient to explain the continued inactivity satisfactorily, rumours were put about that there had been sabotage.

Sabotage? People shook their heads. Why should anyone want to sabotage the flight? And who could have any interest in doing so? Rivals? That was going a bit too far. In the meantime Larre Borges was still receiving weather reports. Good weather, good visibility, but strong winds were forecast. However, the next stage of the flight was only to the Canaries, and as that was a mere hop of not more than 650 miles the risks did not seem very great. Every day the crew of the *Uruguay* would go on board and carry out one or two tests, and then the hydroplane would be left at its moorings again.

People were really beginning to wonder. Even if there had been damage, or even sabotage, the hydroplane should be in order by now. So why was there still no take-off? But then quite suddenly and unexpectedly an end was put to all the rumours and doubts: on March 2nd, 1927, the *Uruguay* took off at dawn and flew away southwards. The third stage of the flight had started.

Las Palmas was the objective of the flight, and the wireless station there had been informed that the *Uruguay* was on its way, and so also had the wireless stations at Safi, Mogador, Ifni and Cape Juby. By the middle of the afternoon none of them had heard anything from the *Uruguay*, but it was a little too early to worry. At 18.00 hours an inquiry was put through to Las Palmas. No, the *Uruguay* hadn't arrived yet. At 19.00 hours the inquiry was repeated—with the same result. At 20.00 hours there was still no news, and then darkness fell. There was real anxiety about the fate of the *Uruguay* and her crew now, and when day dawned and there was still no news it seemed obvious that Larre Borges and his companions must be lost. The *Uruguay* must have come down in the sea.

Astonishment mingled with dismay. Everyone knew that there were still difficulties and dangers connected with any transatlantic flight, but no one had anticipated disaster on the easiest stage of the journey, the stage which Cabral and

Coutinho, Franco and—only a few weeks previously—de Pinedo had flown without the slighest trouble. However, all hope was not yet lost; the *Uruguay* was a hydroplane and would therefore float for a while, provided the seas were not too heavy, so there was every hope that her crew would be rescued, and perhaps the machine itself taken successfully in tow. All vessels sailing the route were alerted, and the Aéropostale machines flying the Toulouse–Dakar line were also engaged in the search.

On March 3rd two gunboats, the *Vanneau* and the *Forfait,* put out on a thorough search of the Rio de Oro and Mauretania coastlines, whilst the pilots of the Aéropostale Line kept a weather eye open over the sands below them in the hope of seeing something of the missing hydroplane or its crew. The dangers that beset anyone in this part of the world were not only the weather and engine failure. If they came down in the sea and managed to make their way ashore safely there was the hostility of the tribes along the coastline.

By March 5th neither the *Vanneau* nor the *Forfait* had found a sign of the flyers or their machine, and none of the pilots on the airline had seen a thing. The authorities were now strongly inclined to abandon the search as useless, particularly since for some days now the sea had been so rough that even if the *Uruguay* had come down safely she could hardly still be afloat. But perhaps there was still a chance over land, so as late as March 6th the two pilots of the Aéropostale plane which left Casablanca at dawn for Cape Juby were told to keep their eyes open for possible survivors.

The long rolling dunes stretched away under the plane's wings, and now and again the pilot would take her down lower to have a closer look at some mound or shadow that had attracted their attention, but always it turned out to have nothing to do with what they still hoped to see. But as they followed the coastline they still searched ceaselessly, staring at the rolling Atlantic on the one side and at the long level stretches of sand on the other.

Jean Mermoz was the name of one of the pilots, a young man of twenty-six, himself destined to be one of the air heroes of the South Atlantic. There was less than a hundred miles to go to Cape Juby, and not a great deal of hope left—unless the survivors of the *Uruguay* had escaped the sea and been captured by rebel tribes along the coast.

'Waddy Chebika,' said his companion Ville, and Mermoz, who was piloting the plane, brought it down so low over the desert that sand and small stones were lifted up by the wind of their flight to rattle against the fuselage. Beneath them was a stony break in the monotonous line of the coast. Mermoz took the plane a little out to sea and then swung round again into the interior, describing smaller and smaller circles over a dark shape below them which had attracted their attention.

'It could be . . .' muttered Ville.

The wreckage of the *Uruguay*, he meant.

'I'm going down to make sure,' said Mermoz, and his companion nodded agreement. They both knew the risk they were taking. Armed Moors could fire on them from hiding as they had often fired on French planes which had flown low, but their job was to look for any signs of Larre Borges and his crew, and they were determined to find out for certain whether what they had glimpsed below them . . .

The plane landed a little way from the entrance to the waddy and the two men sprang down, leaving the propeller of their plane still swinging so that they could take off again quickly in case of attack. They hurried towards the shape they had seen, and there was no doubt about it now: it was the wreckage of a plane. When they were closer they could see that it was a hydroplane, half buried in the sand. The wings were snapped off. On its rump they saw the painted name *Uruguay*. The search for the hydroplane was over. But where were those who had flown it?

A closer examination revealed no signs of life—or death, fortunately. In the sand were the traces of footsteps, though that did not necessarily mean that anyone had survived. They could be the traces of pillaging Arabs, because beyond all doubt the hydroplane had been pillaged, as the débris scattered around showed clearly.

'If they're still alive—or any of them—they're being held by the Moors,' said Mermoz. He happened to know what that meant from personal experience. Towards the end of 1925 he had himself been captured by Moors, and had remained in their hands for nine days: long tramps under the burning sun, rough treatment and insufficient food and drink. And he was lucky to have been ransomed . . .

'If they are alive they're a long way from here now,' he went on. 'For the moment there's nothing we can do for them but get on as quickly as possible and report.'

As soon as they told their story at Cape Juby the Spanish authorities despatched a gunboat, the *Bonifacio* to the spot. A party of sailors landed at the waddy, and found some peaceable Arabs who confirmed that the aviators had been captured by Moors; but more than that they could not, or would not, say.

Shortly after the *Uruguay* flew over Mogador, the mechanic Rigoli was munching a sandwich when he spotted suspicious patches of oil on the cowling. Hurriedly finishing his sandwich he crawled into the engine pit to investigate. When he clambered out again his face was smeary and his hands were covered with oil.

'Broken feed-pipe,' he said laconically.

Larre Borges knew at once that he would have to set his machine down without loss of time whilst he still had power in the engines. About half a mile to port he could see the waves of the Atlantic breaking heavily on the rocky shore. 'There's nothing for it,' he thought. 'I can't save the plane now. In fact we'll be lucky if we can save ourselves.'

He brought the hydroplane down cautiously towards the sea, searching anxiously for a calmer spot in which to set down. Before he could find one a sudden squall hit the machine and forced it down on to the surface so roughly that the struts supporting the engines gave way and one of the propellers ripped into the hull.

The four men stared in the direction of the coast, which seemed to have disappeared, hidden from their eyes at sea level by the white crests of the waves. They were almost beginning to wonder whether the sight of it had been a mirage and that in reality they were still in the middle of the ocean. But then Ibarra climbed out on to one of the wings, and standing upright he could see the coast and the mouth of a waddy.

Things might have been worse: at least the rear engine was still running, and the blades of the propeller it was driving were churning up the water like a ship's screw and slowly sending the *Uruguay* inshore towards safety. She was a wreck, but she was still afloat. Ibarra continued to report their progress, but as they came inshore the swell grew heavier and there was a sudden crash. Ibarra lost his balance and fell backwards on to his chief. For a moment or two the shock numbed them, but then, helping each other, they managed to get ashore safely.

An hour later the four men were sitting wrapped in blankets drinking tea, the prisoners of a band of 150 Moors into whose hands they had fallen. None of the airmen knew anything about this part of the world, and at first they did not realize their plight. With some amusement they watched their captors sharing the booty. One of them had a pair of silk pyjama trousers, another had an accumulator he had wrenched out of its place—no doubt in the belief that it contained some sort of treasure. A third was eagerly fingering a cheque-book, obviously mistaking the cheques for money.

After a while the flyers were roughly dragged to their feet, and with bound hands they were set to march, dragged along at the rear of a camel. It was then they realized for the first time that they were prisoners, and that their fate was uncertain, for no one seemed to understand their questions or be willing to answer them. After a long march with aching feet and parched tongues they finally came to a halt, and they were then made to lie down in the sand and a covering was put over them.

It was a temporary halt. Their captors had spotted a plane, a Goliath from the base at Casablanca called up by the Spanish gunboat *Bonifacio*. It circled over the caravan for a while and then flew away northwards. Had the observer seen anything before they were covered up with that sheet? Larre Borges shrugged his shoulders. At least there was hope; they were obviously being looked for. Sooner or later the wreck of the *Uruguay* would be found, and in any case the Moors themselves would not leave the authorities in doubt for long—they would want the biggest ransom they could possibly get.

In fact the Moors lost no time in getting into touch with the Spanish commandant at Puerto Cansado and demanding ransom money. The negotiations did not take long, for the number of planes involved in the hunt told the Moors that the airmen were really important, and that sooner or later they would have to give up their prisoners. Two days later a plane landed near the encampment of the kidnappers. A shot or two was fired, but the two pilots who descended were waving a white flag. They had brought the ransom demanded. That same evening the crew of the ill-fated *Uruguay* were safe and sound at Cape Juby.

The pilots of the Aéropostale Line had played a leading part in rescuing the crew of the *Uruguay*, and before long they were to fly regularly over the route which those first pioneers had flown at the risk of their lives.

Ten days later, on March 18th, a hydroplane piloted by Sarmiento de Beires, with a Portuguese crew, set down at Natal coming from Fernando Noronha. But so far no one had succeeded in crossing the South Atlantic in direct flight.

A Frenchman named Saint Romans studied the challenging problem from all angles, and decided to try the hop with a two-engined Farman converted into a hydroplane. On May 5th he set off from St. Louis du Senegal with a crew of two, Mouneyres and Petit. Nothing more was ever heard of them, but a month later a float belonging to their plane was found in the sea; if there had been any doubt as to their fate it was set at rest.

French airmen were the first victims of the attempt to fly the South Atlantic, and they were to be the first victims of the attempt to fly the Atlantic from east to west, for three days after the disappearance of Saint Romans and his crew the two French airmen Nungesser and Coli set off from Le Bourget in the *L'Oseau Blanc*.

4

Nungesser and Coli

A sports car pulled up in front of a small hotel near the Gare du Nord. It was past midnight, and the streets were deserted. The two men in the car looked up for a moment at the dark, silent façade.

'He must be still asleep,' said one of them.

The driver sounded the horn once or twice.

'He sleeps soundly once he's off,' remarked his companion, a man of about thirty-five with a scarred face.

'Shall I go in and fetch him?'

'Sound your horn again a bit.'

The driver sounded the horn vigorously, and the two of them shouted up at the window. After a while a light appeared in one of them and it was opened.

'All right! All right!' a man in his shirt-sleeves called out. 'I'll be down in a minute.'

'I should think so, too,' retorted scar-face. 'Do you want us to go without you?' And he burst into a roar of laughter which sounded a trifle forced, and which stopped dead as a couple of policemen loomed up with a 'What's all this about?' sort of air.

'What do you think you're doing with that horn of yours?' one of them demanded. 'Do you want to wake up the whole neighbourhood? People want to sleep at this time of night.'

'Sorry, constable. We're going to fly the Atlantic, you see.'

'Oh, very funny! Well you mind you're a bit quieter about it or I can tell you where you'll fly.'

And with that the two policemen walked sedately on. As

a matter of fact, one of the men in the car, and the man at the window were about to make a certain amount of noise in the world. The man with the scarred face was Charles Nungesser, and the man he had come to knock up was his friend and companion Coli; it was true that the pair of them now proposed to fly from Paris to New York, crossing the Atlantic from east to west in one hop—for the first time.

In May 1926 a small group of men accompanied one of their friends to the pier in New York Harbour where a liner was about to leave for Le Havre. The passenger was a Frenchman, a man who had become rather popular in the United States during his stay—'As an acrobat of the air', as he put it himself, perhaps a trifle bitterly. He had been the hero of a series of aerobatics during which he recalled the duels he had fought with German pilots for four long years over the fields of France during the Great War. He had emerged victorious from such mortal combats on no less than forty-five occasions. 'The most sensational air attraction of the age,' the programmes used to say, and Nungesser's air displays had certainly been a popular attraction. Whilst in the United States he married a descendant of the famous John Augustus Sutter, the man who had 'put California on the map' and had made the first dis-covery which led to the gold rush which finally ruined him. Nungesser was now returning to France, after having made a film 'The Sky-Raiders'.

His brother Robert, who had settled in Washington, was one of the group seeing him off.

'Good-bye, chaps,' said Charles Nungesser cheerily. 'I'm going home to Paris the slow way, but I'll come back to New York the fast way next time—by plane.'

Nungesser had been bitten by the transatlantic flight bug. He was not the only one. In France Tarascon had also put his name down for the 25,000-dollar prize offered by the French-born U.S. citizen, Raymond B. Orteig, for a non-stop New

York to Paris or Paris to New York transatlantic flight, though public attention was directed chiefly to another World War ace, René Fonck, who was in New York preparing to attempt a transatlantic flight with a three-engined Sikorski biplane. However, Fonck's departure was continually delayed by various disputes. French public opinion began to get impatient. There was a rumour that the Germans were making preparations for a transatlantic flight too, and they mustn't be allowed to get ahead.

On September 17th, everything was ready for the start, but at the last moment a mechanic noticed patches of oil on the engine cowling—a broken feed pipe, and the flight had to be postponed. There was very little time left now: summer was over, autumn was at hand, and in another couple of weeks all thought of a transatlantic flight would have to be abandoned until the following year.

Impatient telegrams began to arrive for Fonck. 'Start, at least—even if you have to come down in the sea!' advised his colleague Weiss. In the meantime Fonck worked hard to get his machine ready again, and on September 20th he arrived on Mitchell airfield, wearing the uniform of the French Air Force. After examining his machine and going into conference with its Polish constructor Sikorski he announced that he would leave the following morning.

At dawn the next day the plane was wheeled out of its hangar and taken to a specially constructed runway which could stand the weight of the plane with its extra weight of petrol—an overall burden of eleven and a half tons—which was tremendous for those days. Fonck and his crew of three climbed on board, the engines roared, the propellers began to turn and then the plane started its run. The first attempt to cross the Atlantic non-stop from New York to Paris had started. Rapidly the plane increased speed . . .

'I was just looking at my watch,' explained one of the spectators afterwards, 'when I thought the sun must have risen very quickly. There was a sudden glow and I saw it light up the face of Sikorski, who was standing next to me. He opened his mouth as though to shout. Flames were leaping into the air now, bordered by black smoke. Fonck's plane was on fire.'

Cars raced towards the scene of the conflagration, and two figures were seen staggering away from the flaming plane. They were René Fonck and Curtis, one of the members of his crew. The remaining two were unable to make their escape, and were burned to death.

Nungesser eagerly read everything that was written about the disaster. Of course Fonck would try again, and he, Nungesser, regretted that he was not in the running himself. Incidentally he had suffered that sort of crash too—and he hadn't got off as lightly as Fonck. It has been on January 29th, 1916; when they had pulled him out of the wreckage of his machine both his legs had been broken, his jaw had been fractured and also his palate and skull.

They had wanted to invalid him out after that, but Nungesser was determined not to let them, and within a comparatively short time he was in the air again fighting over Verdun. In 1918, just after the war, he took part in the annual swim across Paris—just to demonstrate to wounded ex-Service men that they were far from finished even when they had suffered severe injuries.

His mind was on the Paris to New York trip now. It would be no easy job: forty hours at least in the air without sleep, and hardly able to stretch. All the time he would have to keep not only awake but alert, resisting the cold and fatigue, and fighting against the wind, drift, icing, and whatever other dangers might arise. Nevertheless he felt he could do it—in fact he was sure he could do it. But with what sort of machine?

Aviation had made a good deal of progress since the war, and there were quite a number of machines with a range which would take them over the Atlantic—on paper at least. There was one in particular whose plans had been submitted to him. It was a big monoplane with hollow wings which would allow the inspection of the engines during the flight. The cockpit was enclosed, and the machine could carry a big reserve of petrol. On the other hand it was going to be very expensive, and Nungesser, like a good many other men of action, was not wealthy. There was another disadvantage, too: a big plane like that would require a crew, and he really preferred doing things on his own. It was better that way, he felt: you took all the risks yourself, and when you made your decisions you had no one else to consider—which made things easier. No, it would have to be a smaller plane, a lighter plane, and one that wouldn't cost so much. Perhaps his friends at the Air Ministry could help him. He applied to them, but he received a disappointing answer. For the time being the Minister could not see his way clear to finance or support such an undertaking.

Nungesser found himself baulked at every turn, and he was beginning to feel depressed. In addition, he was on his own, for his wife had returned to the States. But Nungesser was not easy to get down, and he had been in difficult spots before. One of them had been in the Argentine, when, as a very young man, he had gone in search of adventure and to find an uncle who was reputed to own a hacienda. One evening he had been to a boxing match between a Frenchman and a local Argentinian champion. Unfortunately the Frenchman had been knocked out by a left jab to the stomach in the very first round. Such things do happen, and that might have been the end of that, but the Argentinian had not taken his swift victory modestly, and had made some offensive remark about his enemy's nationality. Promptly Nungesser had risen in his seat, determined to demonstrate that Frenchmen were anything but cowards. The Argentinian had looked him up and down. Nungesser was wiry and muscular, but he weighed perhaps ten stone whilst his opponent weighed at least thirteen.

Nungesser had been given some ring togs, and the fight had begun. At first the Argentinian, heavier and more experienced, had had the best of it. He had put the Frenchman down three times, but each time Nungesser had been on his feet again, plugging away indomitably. His spirit and courage had quickly won the admiration and support of the audience, though they were all Argentinians. They had cheered him on wildly and it was quite obvious that whatever the outcome of the unequal struggle the reputation of Frenchmen for courage was established in their eyes beyond all doubt.

Nungesser had been floored no less than fifteen times during the course of the battle, and each time he had bobbed up again and fought on. There had been a sixteenth knock-down in that fight, but it was not Nungesser who measured his length this time, but the Argentinian. Nungesser had caught him on the point with a beautiful right hook to the chin, and it had been a haymaker. The Argentinian had gone down for the count, and as the referee raised Nungesser's gloved hand the audience had jumped up in their seats and gone wild over the gallant Frenchman's unexpected victory. Battered and bleeding, the plucky Nungesser had grinned happily at the enthusiastic Argentinians and acknowledged their applause and cheering.

He was not a conceited man, but when he was up against it he liked to recall that little adventure. Right, so the Air Ministry wouldn't help? Very well, he'd try the aircraft firms. After all, what a wonderful piece of publicity for the firm whose plane he piloted across the Atlantic! The first man he tried was Pierre Levasseur—in his office in the Avenue Félix Faure.

'I want a plane to fly across the Atlantic from east to west,' he said bluntly.

'Oh, you do, do you? I take it you know what you're asking for there?'

'Certainly. And I'm quite confident that I can do it.'

'I'm equally certain that you've got all the qualities necessary to do it, but . . .'

'But what? I've no doubt that you've got all the qualities necessary to find me a machine capable of doing it.'

'I'll think it over.'

'There's not much time for that. I need the plane within, say, three months at the outside.'

'Three months!'

'Yes, at the outside. The Americans are getting ready now and I don't want them to get in first.'

'I see. Now what about the financial side of it?'

'I'm broke.'

Pierre Lavasseur looked at his visitor thoughtfully. There was no mistaking the air of decision and confidence about the man, but he was asking a good deal: an aeroplane capable of flying the Atlantic, within three months—and without a sou to finance the job.

'Look,' said Nungesser, 'amongst the planes you design and build there must be one suitable.'

'You're thinking of a hydroplane, I suppose?'

'No, I'm not. Too heavy. And very difficult to get into the air with sufficient petrol.'

'But in the event of engine failure—'

'I want to fly the Atlantic, not sail it, or I'd take the boat.'

'How many engines do you reckon?'

'It's a small plane I want. A big plane requires too much petrol; and in any case, I want to do the job on my own.'

'On your own!'

'That's right.'

Pierre Levasseur thought in silence for a while. Despite what Nungesser said he thought that a hydroplane would be better for the job. But he was already half-won over by Nungesser's determination.

'Supposing you left Le Bourget in an aeroplane and arrived in New York in a hydroplane?'

'What do you mean exactly?'

Pierre Levasseur laughed.

'The fact is that at the moment we're building certain special machines for the Navy . . .'

'Amphibians?'

'Not exactly. They're no heavier than ordinary planes, but

their fuselage is so designed that they float if they have to come down on the water. In addition the undercarriage can be discarded, which means less weight and therefore less petrol. How long do you reckon you would need to stay in the air?'

'Forty hours at least.'

'It could be done.'

'And what about speed?'

'Maximum 125 miles an hour, but fully loaded the cruising speed wouldn't be more than a hundred.'

Nungesser made rapid calculations. That would give him a range of 4,000 miles. The distance from Paris to New York was 3,500 miles. The margin wasn't very big.

'Is forty hours the maximum time the machine could stay in the air?'

'Well, I think you could reasonably reckon with forty-two.'

'That would give me another couple of hundred miles to spare,' said Nungesser. 'Right. It'll do. Let me have the navy plane, then.'

'You wouldn't like more time to think it over?'

'No. I've already thought it over.'

'Very well. Come back in a few days. I'll have to get permission from the Admiralty, you know.'

The two men rose and shook hands, and Nungesser left the offices of the famous designer with a radiant face. He had done it; he had got hold of a plane capable of taking him over the Atlantic to New York.

René Fonck was in France again looking for engines to fly the new Sikorski with which he proposed to try again.

'Do you think you'll be ready before your rivals?' a journalist wanted to know.

'What do you think we are?' Fonck demanded irritably. 'Racehorses lined up at the gate? We're going to fly the Atlantic, that's all. Whoever's ready first will start first—and good luck to him. It won't make the job any less difficult for those who start after him—or less important.'

That was a very dignified attitude to adopt, but the fact remained that whether they liked it or not, the men who proposed to fly the Atlantic were racing—and the race was worth 25,000 dollars to the first man who linked Paris and New York non-stop by air. And to add to the interest, the *Matin* published the names of those who had declared their intention of making the attempt. It was quite a list. First of all there was Commander, afterwards Admiral Byrd, who had flown over the Pole with his friend Floyd Bennet the previous year. Then there was Noel Davis, Lieutenant Wade, René Fonck himself, and a certain Charles Lindenburg—this afterwards turned out to be a misprint; the young man's name was Lindbergh. And proposing to do the same flight, but in the opposite direction, were an Italian named Bernardi, and no less than three Frenchmen: Drouhin, Tarascon, and Coli.

Nungesser's name was not on the list, but he was making his preparations—without publicity, but with great thoroughness and determination. For one thing he had gone back to school, and he was a very industrious pupil. He was studying meteorology, wireless navigation and everything connected with the piloting of a plane across the Atlantic. Moreover he regularly visited the machine that was being prepared for him under the supervision of a brilliant aero-engineer named Farret. The navy plane was being adapted to his use, special reserve tanks were being added, the stabilizers and ailerons were being modified—and the precise amount of petrol which could be carried was being calculated down to the last drop. It was no easy job, for Nungesser wanted the maximum possible amount of fuel for the minimum possible amount of weight.

'Fuel comes first,' he insisted. 'Everything must be sacrificed to that. Unless I can carry enough petrol I can't succeed.'

He had already decided against wireless. It was too heavy; the corresponding weight of petrol would be worth more.

'No wireless!' Farret had exclaimed. 'But supposing you

have to come down? You'll need wireless to give your position.'

'My dear Farret, I'm thinking of flying to New York, not of saving my skin. You fly with petrol, not with wireless sets. The weight of the wireless set with its accumulators means so and so many gallons of petrol less. Give me the petrol every time.'

'And what about food and instruments?'

'Yes, of course, but only what's absolutely necessary, and a minimum at that. I'm afraid there'll have to be an inflatable dinghy, though. Coli insists on one. He's an old sailor, you know, and they don't much care for swimming.'

The two men laughed. The fact was that Nungesser had decided not to go alone after all, and had joined forces with Coli. Coli was a man ten years older than himself, a sailor who had taken up flying during the war—and had lost one eye during his service. Since then he had already done one or two noteworthy long-distance flights; on January 26th, 1919, he had made the double crossing of the Mediterranean in twenty-four hours, and four months later he had set up a new record for a flight from Paris to Kenitra. For a long time—since 1924 in fact—he had been thinking about the transatlantic crossing from Paris to New York. At first he had linked up with Tarascon, but then Tarascon gave up the idea temporarily, and Coli had found himself on his own. He had given a great deal of thought to the matter, and he had studied every possible route that came into question. Apart from spending hours and hours poring over maps and charts of the route, he had closely studied the Navigational Almanac, learning everything there was to know about the tides, the prevailing weather and the dominant winds, particularly on the other side of the Atlantic, where a forced landing might have to take place; at the same time he had become a real expert in the use of the sextant and in all the calculations relating to air navigation. Being a thorough man, another thing he had done was to practise keeping awake in the air over the sea for twenty, thirty and more hours. This he had done flying up and down over his native Mediterranean; so when he finally told Nungesser that he was ready, it was no overstatement.

One day they were examining their plane when Coli suggested that she ought to have a name.

'I suppose she ought,' agreed Nungesser. 'They're going to paint her white, so that she'll be easier to find if we have to come down in the sea.'

Coli nodded.

'What about calling her *The White Bird* then?

'Good idea.'

So the plane in which they finally took off on their transatlantic flight from east to west was named *L'Oiseau Blanc*.

Practically every day Nungesser was in the Levasseur workshops. On one occasion the engine had been running in the test pit successfully for twenty-four hours. Nungesser examined the undercarriage. 'Getting her off the ground in the first place with all that fuel-oil on board will be the hardest part,' he thought. He would have to get five tons into the air from a runway not more than half a mile long. The accident which had stopped Fonck's attempt and cost two of his companions their lives bulked large in his mind, though, of course, Fonck's plane had weighed twice as much as *L'Oiseau Blanc*. Still . . . 'Once we're in the air it will be all right.'

On the way home that day he heard newspaper sellers shouting something about an accident to Byrd. Hurriedly Nungesser bought a paper and read the news. Byrd's plane, the one in which he proposed to fly the Atlantic, had crashed when taking off for a training flight. Fortunately Byrd and his crew were uninjured, but the machine had been badly damaged, and it was feared that it could not be got ready in time for a start in May as had been intended.

Byrd had been the favourite for the transatlantic race. It would be Noel Davis now. Nungesser felt no satisfaction at the thought that Byrd was practically out of the running, but

the accident confirmed his own fears about the extra burden
the vast amount of petrol imposed; it made the take-off a real
terror. Byrd, who was a first-class flying man, would have
taken every possible precaution. Resolutely Nungesser turned
on his heel and went back into the Levasseur works.

'Could I take her up tomorrow?'

'Tomorrow! You didn't say anything about that just
now.'

'No I didn't, but can you manage it all the same?'

'Tomorrow's a bit early. The next day, if you insist.'

On the agreed day both Nungesser and Coli were on the
flying field at Villacoublay. They climbed into the cockpit,
checked the controls and made contact. The air propeller,
made specially of duralumin, began to turn. The chocks were
removed and *L'Oiseau Blanc* started to move. She took the air
without difficulty, and Nungesser put her through her paces,
reaching her top speed of 125 miles an hour. She answered the
controls smoothly, and easily performed all the manœuvres
he put her through. When he touched down he was satisfied.
He had a good plane, a first-class tool for the job he had in
hand.

The next day he took her up again with three tons of petrol,
and then with four.

'It's going to be all right,' he said to the mechanics when
he landed.

'Won't you try her with the full load?'

'No. When I do, either we'll get off or we shan't; and the
day's soon enough to find that out. If I try and succeed, then
I've done the one big job uselessly, and I shall only have to do
it again on the day. No, once is enough. It's no use challenging
the gods.'

'What about the engine?'

'Nothing wrong with it that I could discover.'

'We've got a replacement ready. It's going through a
forty-hour non-stop test in the pit now.'

'Good.'

Before going into a café with Coli back in Paris he bought a newspaper. It told him that Noel Davis, whose last bulletin had said that he would be leaving on his transatlantic flight 'at any moment now', had crashed with his plane, the *American Legion*, taking off for a final test, and been killed.

For a moment or two there was silence.

'Anything else?' asked Coli.

'Yes, there's a report that those two fellows Nungesser and Coli are starting at the end of the month.'

'That's nice,' said Coli. 'I'm glad you mentioned it; I might have made other arrangements.'

The waiter came up.

'M. Nungesser, several gentlemen were here to see you. They couldn't wait any longer, but they said they'd be back in half an hour.'

'Thanks, but I don't know whether I'll be here that long.'

'Who are they?' asked Coli. 'Do you know?'

'Yes. They're from newspapers and magazines, offering us contracts for exclusive articles, interviews and so on when we've flown the Atlantic.'

'Why don't they wait till we have?'

'That's what I told them. But at least people seem to have noticed that I still exist, which is something. And it's beginning to look as though we shall be the first after all.'

In the meantime opinions on his chances of success were divided. 'Oh, Nungesser'll do it all right,' was the confident belief of the average Frenchman. 'He knows what he's up to.' But there were others, who knew more about the risks involved: a flight of 3,600 miles over the Atlantic in a plane with a radius of action of about 4,000 miles. It was a very small margin. The one engine could break down; the compass could get out of order; the navigator could make a mistake; a feed pipe could leak; or the weather could prove unfavourable after all—fogs, adverse winds, storms. 'The odds are against him,' they murmured, 'even if he manages to get a heavily loaded plane off the ground in the first place.'

On April 26th the *Petit Parisien* reported that *L'Oiseau Blanc* was about to leave at any moment.

'What do you want to leave me in the dark for?' grumbled Coli. 'Or maybe you don't know anything about it either. But no, you've obviously given it up in favour of the lightweight championship.'

Nungesser was, in fact, doing a rapid turn at the punching ball.

'Splendid way to keep fit, *mon ami*. We've got to stay awake for forty hours at least—and keep alert the whole time too. You can't be off-colour for that. Not that I've really any doubts.'

Nungesser took off the gloves, had a shower and dressed.

'Did you get in touch with the weather men?'

'I did. I told them we should be needing regular reports from May 1st on.'

The meteorological reports were their bugbear now. Everything else was ready. Coli had carefully planned their route: across the Channel, along the south coast of England, across the Bristol Channel to Southern Ireland—and then out to sea, more or less along the 54th parallel to Newfoundland—and then south to New York. The experts had not failed to point out that the east to west crossing was more difficult than the opposite direction—the only direction in which the Atlantic had been crossed by a plane in one hop so far. There were constant adverse winds to be reckoned with when flying westward.

'The old windjammers managed it, all the same,' objected Coli. 'They tacked, didn't they? Well, so will we.'

That was not meant all too seriously. Both Nungesser and Coli knew perfectly well that the east–west crossing was, in fact, very much more difficult. But if they went to the U.S.A. and flew the Atlantic from west to east it would be like visiting themselves. Let the Americans do it that way to visit France. Frenchmen just had to fly the other way to visit the States. The western winds would have to be fair to moderate, and not too strong; of course, an east wind to help them on their way would be better still.

'It happens sometimes,' said the weather experts, 'but not very often. However . . .'

On May 4th they received two items of news. One was that Chamberlain and Levine were starting off that day on their transatlantic attempt—and the second was that there had been a fire at Villacoublay, and that the *L'Oiseau Blanc* had almost been destroyed. Fortunately it turned out that the actual damage to their plane was very slight and could easily be made good; the only real trouble was that the canvas had been scorched here and there. And that evening a cable announced that the two American flyers had postponed their attempt after all on account of bad weather.

'Yes,' confirmed the meteorologists. 'There is mist and fog over there, particularly over Newfoundland, but an anti-cyclone is forming in the North Atlantic.'

'Which means that we stand a chance of taking off the next forty-eight hours?'

'It's possible.'

They were cautious, those experts, and unwilling to commit themselves.

On Friday, May 7th, *L'Oiseau Blanc* flew from Villacoublay to Le Bourget. The compass was checked and everything was made ready. To decrease the danger of fire it was decided not to tank up with the full load of petrol until the last moment. Nungesser and Coli went back to Paris and paid another visit to the Avenue Rapp, where the meteorological office was situated.

'The weather over Newfoundland is still bad,' they were informed. 'But it's not so bad as it was, and there's a hope of continued improvement. In fact for the first third, say, of your journey you can even hope for east winds.'

The hopes of the two men rose.

'East winds, Coli!' exclaimed Nungesser eagerly. 'The fabulous east winds you daren't even hope for in the ordinary way.'

Coli had heard, and he guessed that Nungesser had decided to start. At dawn on Sunday was the actual moment.

The next day Nungesser had lunch in his mother's little flat on the Boulevard Voltaire as usual.

'One of your favourite meals, Charles,' she said as she kissed him, 'with *pommes frites*, and *crème au chocolat* to follow.'

That day Nungesser seemed even more cheerful and affectionate than usual. He was probably feeling relieved that the decision was very near at last. After having coffee with his mother he got up to go.

'You're always dashing off somewhere or other,' she complained. 'And how's this famous aeroplane of yours getting on? You've never even shown it to me. I've got a feeling you'll be going off with Coli before long.'

'For the mother of an airman you're a bit naïve. Look at the weather! You couldn't fly far in this. I'll still be here on your birthday, you see.'

Madame Nungesser's birthday was on the thirtieth. She went out on to the landing to wave good-bye to him.

'You'll be coming back?' she called out as he ran down the stairs, and the tears were unbidden in her eyes.

'Of course,' he called back. 'I'm one of those who always turn up—like a bad penny.'

Down below he hailed a taxi: 'Number eighteen, Avenue Rapp,' he said.

He had arranged to meet Coli at the meteorological office, and Coli was there when he arrived. The experts were encouraging. There was a gradual improvement of the weather over the Atlantic. Local storms were to be expected in Northern France, but nothing very serious. Unfortunately there was still thick fog over Newfoundland.

Nungesser was disinclined to take the fog risk too seriously. 'After all,' he thought, 'if it's too bad we can always fly on over Canada. And we shall have flown the Atlantic from east to west even if we don't get straight to New York.' It was worth risking. He was probably thinking of this when on

April 26th he put his name down, not for the non-stop Paris to New York flight, but for the long-distance record flight.

'We'll come back at half-past five,' he said to Coli, 'and see what the situation is then. Get your things ready, anyway.'

At half-past five that evening Nungesser, Coli and Pierre Levasseur were in the office of General Delcambre, the head of the Meteorological Service. On the wall was a large-scale chart of the North Atlantic with the latest meteorological graphs.

'Well, *mon Général*?' queried Nungesser.

'The improvement we forecast is developing,' replied the General. 'And I can also tell you that for about twelve hundred miles or so of the crossing you should have the wind behind you.'

'Good! And after that?'

'Things become a little uncertain, and I can't tell you anything with any degree of confidence. The weather broadcasts from OXF Greenland are inaudible, and so we don't know for certain how things are going in the north-west.'

'Are conditions for the first twelve hundred miles likely to remain unchanged?' asked Pierre Levasseur thoughtfully.

'Not for long. And that's the most I can tell you, messieurs. It's up to you to decide.'

Nungesser, Coli and Pierre Levasseur left the weather bureau. The two flyers then parted from Levasseur, and walked on through the crowded Saturday evening streets in silence for a while. Both of them were thinking hard.

'Well, Coli, what do you say?' Nungesser asked finally.

'He said conditions were favourable at the moment, but not likely to last. Perhaps we ought to take advantage of them.'

'You're for starting, then?'

'Yes.'

'Right.'

In the street the two men, relieved that the decision had at last been taken, shook each other warmly by the hand. A quick conference at 10.00 hours that evening with Levasseur and a number of others, and it was arranged that they should take off from Le Bourget the following morning at dawn.

The news spread like wildfire, and by midnight there was a crowd of people waiting at the aerodrome. What exactly they hoped to see it was difficult to say—perhaps Nungesser and Coli making their final preparations. But, in fact, they found the whole place silent, the hangars closed, and all entrances guarded by soldiers who let no one through except those with special passes: employees of the aerodrome, officials and special friends of the two flyers.

As the night wore on 'all Paris' seemed to have a rendezvous on the well-worn grass of the aerodrome, and when the after-theatre suppers were over and the night clubs closing down the crowd grew as though for a gala première. And so it was: the curtain was about to go up on a drama, but no one as yet knew whether it was going to be a tragedy or a triumph.

In the meantime the crowd kept itself amused by spotting celebrities—and there were many of them there: Maurice Chevalier; Mistinguett; the famous French boxer Georges Carpentier; Tristan Bernard, and a good many others. Nungesser and Coli were not to be seen. They were trying to get a few hours sleep on camp beds in the aerodrome building. The remains of their supper were on a plain wooden table near by. Around them mechanics and others talked in low tones in order not to disturb them, and there was a strong smell of fresh petrol, because in a nearby hangar *L'Oiseau Blanc* was being tanked up with her full load: 880 gallons precisely.

The men who were doing the job were trying to keep their minds off what would happen if *L'Oiseau Blanc* crashed at the take-off with all that high-octane aviation spirit on board . . . Without saying anything to the two flyers, the aerodrome chief had arranged for fire engines and an ambulance to be in waiting at the end of the runway—for all eventualities.

Finally, the two men got up. Nungesser's face was serious, but Coli was trying to dissipate the tension by studied light-heartedness. As the time for the take-off approached, two representatives of the Aero Club put seals on the control instruments; for the performance was to be carefully checked and would have to be ratified officially before it could go down in the international records.

Provisions were taken on board—three tins of tunny fish, a tin of sardines, a couple of pounds of sugar, a dozen bananas, biscuits, chocolate, two quarts of hot coffee in thermos flasks, and some brandy. At the last moment they had decided to take no reserves, but only just enough for the forty hours or so they expected to be in the air. And there were no life-saving jackets. Even Coli's inflatable rubber dinghy had been sacrificed in their desperate efforts to work out that vital equation: the maximum amount of petrol compared with the minimum amount of weight. 'Just a small gadget for distilling sea water,' said Coli. 'And a hook and line to catch cod—what else?—off Cape Cod.'

He laughed, and Nungesser smiled for the first time. He looked at his wrist-watch: half-past three.

'I'll just get Cortichiato to give me a final massage, and then we'll get into our flying togs,' he said.

Cortichiato, a medical friend, massaged him and gave him an injection of caffeine. Then they put on their special flying combinations, which were of bright yellow and very warm, and Coli carefully tucked his old flying licence away in an inside pocket—for luck—and a comb, 'to make myself handsome when we arrive and not disappoint the girls'.

Finally they were ready.

'We look more as though we're going deep-sea diving in this rig-out,' said the irrepressible Coli.

And now the doors of the hangar were opened and the fully tanked L'Oiseau Blanc was rolled off to the runway.

'Well, Coli?' asked Nungesser quietly. 'All set and still of the same mind?'

'Absolutely,' said Coli.

Impulsively Nungesser hugged his comrade.

'Right then; let's get going,' he said.

Suddenly there was a strange sound that grew in volume; for the moment they thought it was a storm of rain beating on the tin roofs of the hangars, but it turned out to be the crowd stamping their feet in unison as *L'Oiseau Blanc* was wheeled down to the start.

The time had come for leave-takings, and Coli and Nungesser shook hands with their friends. Nungesser was very serious again. 'You know what the thing means,' he said. 'We're taking a risk, I know, but we're taking it willingly. With all our hearts.' And turning to General Girod, the man who had given him his first plane during the war: 'General,' he said, 'if we shouldn't make it, then I'm relying on you to bear witness to the fact that we took no unnecessary risks and that we prepared our flight as carefully as it possibly could have been prepared.'

'I know. I know. But you're going to make it,' said the General, deeply moved.

'Yes, I think so,' agreed Nungesser. 'At least we're going to do our best. Right, Coli: off we go.'

The two of them in their flying kit now got into the back seat of an open sporting car and were driven down to where *L'Oiseau Blanc* was waiting to take off. For the first time the crowds spotted the two flyers and there was a roar of cheering. A young woman tossed a rose to Nungesser, who caught it in the air and blew her a kiss.

It was ten minutes past five when they prepared to climb into their plane. Nungesser shook hands again with a few intimate friends and hugged his brother. Then he climbed into the cockpit. Just as Coli was about to follow him an orderly hurried up with a message: the latest weather forecast. Coli read it, and Nungesser, who had noticed the little incident, looked down. 'Anything important?'

'No. A minor trough of depression is beginning to form. We shall have to alter course a little farther northward to avoid it; that's all. That is to say, if you're in agreement?'

Nungesser nodded and the two of them took their places in

the plane. There was a fire somewhere to the west, and on the horizon there were flashes of lightning as a storm beat up. Nungesser made contact, and at 05.18 hours the air-screw began to turn. The engine was giving off little mauve flames. Nungesser let it run for a while and then he gave the signal that he was ready. The mechanics pulled away the chocks and *L'Oiseau Blanc* began to move.

On the ground Pierre Levasseur, Farret, General Girod and the others who knew that the take-off was the first big difficulty to be overcome stared anxiously as *L'Oiseau Blanc* gathered speed. 'Once we can get her off the ground it will be all right,' Nungesser had said more than once. Five tons had to be lifted into the air by an engine of 450 h.p., within less than half a mile. The expert watchers thought of the pneumatic tyres bursting under the friction, or the undercarriage collapsing under the weight . . .

Inside the plane Nungesser was at the controls and looking out with concentrated attention. Before they came to the end of the runway they must take off—or crash.

'She's off the ground!' someone shouted. And in fact *L'Oiseau Blanc* had leapt off the ground for a moment; but then she fell back. The grey light of dawn was strengthening now, and the watchers could see the remaining length of runway growing shorter. *L'Oiseau Blanc* leapt into the air again, and again she returned to the ground, still speeding on. The end of the runway was not more than a couple of hundred yards or so away now, and the watchers felt their mouths going dry in their intense anxiety: success or disaster was a matter of seconds, and men found themselves clenching their fists. There was dead silence, and then suddenly at the last moment it happened: *L'Oiseau Blanc* rose from the ground, cleared a line of trees beyond the airfield, gained height, remained visible for a while, and then disappeared into the twilight.

For a moment or two the silence continued and no one moved. The thing they had all been waiting months for, even years—the take-off of a plane from Paris to fly to New York—

had happened at last, and now a ragged cheer rose and grew in volume for the two gallant men who were already too far away to hear it.

Then the threatening storm broke. There was a flash of lightning, a long roll of thunder, and the rain began to pelt down. At that there was a concerted move, and people began to run for cover.

A special edition of *La Presse* was issued in the evening on May 9th, 1927. In a banner headline it announced the success of Nungesser and Coli, and there followed a description of the scene in New York on their arrival. Commandant Foullois, the commander of the fighters stationed around New York had ordered out a squadron to escort *L'Oiseau Blanc* to the airfield; all the ships in New York harbour had set their sirens blowing; and the French and American flags were hoisted on all buildings. Many waiting pleasure boats had put out into the harbour with sightseers to look at the French machine lying on the water of the harbour, whilst in the sky above planes carrying cameramen were recording the scene for the newsreels, and newspaper men were taking photographs for the press.

Those who read this marvellous scoop in *La Presse*, were told that Nungesser had put down *L'Oiseau Blanc* on the surface of the harbour without the slightest difficulty and under very favourable conditions. At first the two men had sat there as though spellbound by their success, and then they had stood up and hugged each other for joy. A motor-boat had then drawn alongside and taken the two gallant flyers ashore, where they were welcomed by wildly cheering crowds and smothered with ticker-tape.

People in France were wildly excited, too. So they had really done it! And right on time! They had touched down as planned at one o'clock in the afternoon, with the precision of a railway time-table. Within a hundred yards of the Statue of Liberty, the newspaper added for good measure. People in high places and the man in the street were equally pleased. 'I knew Nungesser would do it,' an ex-soldier exclaimed joy-fully, and to celebrate the victory he pinned up all his medals. 'I served with him during the war. That was a fellow, I can tell you!'

The enthusiasm and relief was shared by the crowds every-where, on the streets, in the underground, on the trams, in shops and offices and in factories and workshops. As soon as they got the news they poured out on to the boulevards as they have done to celebrate all great events throughout French history, as they crowded the streets on Armistice Day, for example, and as they were to crowd the streets on Liberation Day.

Then it was announced that as soon as the arrival was officially confirmed, salvos would be fired from the Invalides and from Fort Vincennes, and that a military aeroplane would fly over the capital firing rocket signals. A plane actually appeared through the drizzle of fine rain which was unable to dampen the spirits of the enthusiastic crowds, and it was firing rocket signals!

At that very moment in New York the Statue of Liberty in New York Harbour could be seen only through the mist. Moored near it was a hydroplane whose nose rose and fell in a heavy swell, but it was an American machine and not *L'Oiseau Blanc*. On the quayside the American flyer Lieutenant Wade, and Robert Nungesser, another brother of the French aviator, were looking out with binoculars in the hope of spotting *L'Oiseau Blanc*. But there was no sign of her.

This was odd, because agency messages had said that she had been sighted over Cape Race in Newfoundland, and then again over Newbury and Boston, though the big New York dailies, the *New York Times* for example, had so far been unable to obtain any confirmation. The waiting newspaper-men were even beginning to ask themselves whether their agency colleagues had been dreaming. But they had not been dreaming: an aeroplane had actually passed over as reported—but it had not been *L'Oiseau Blanc*.

From midday on observers between New York and Halifax were on the look-out for the French plane, and at Portland, Boston, Cape Cod and Nantucket—all places where the navigator Coli might well be on the look-out to find his bearings—many pilots took their machines into the air to meet *L'Oiseau Blanc* and escort her in. There were private planes, sport planes, military and naval planes, and the hydroplanes of the Coast Guard Service. One plane in particular was in the air, though not for the same purpose; it was the hydroplane of the Italian flyer de Pinedo, who had flown across the South Atlantic and reached New York by stages. He had taken off to fly to Philadelphia just at the time that Nungesser and Coli were expected, but as the mist thickened he experienced trouble which compelled him to touch down about thirty miles from New York. Numerous eager watchers immediately reported that *L'Oiseau Blanc* had arrived.

No confirmation was obtainable, and then denials began to come through. Nungesser and Coli had not arrived, and nothing was known of their whereabouts. In the meantime the weather had become very bad indeed, but a squadron of U.S. military planes nevertheless set out from Boston in the hope of meeting *L'Oiseau Blanc*.

Back in Paris there were anxious moments in the newspaper offices. By this time it was known that the earlier reports were untrue, but the crowds on the streets, still gay and cheerful and still cheering the victory of Nungesser and Coli, did not know. The newspapermen waited as long as they could, but finally they had to pour cold water on the enthusiasm, and in newspaper-office windows appeared a laconic message: 'No official confirmation is obtainable of the reported arrival of Nungesser and Coli in New York.' At first the crowds were stupefied, and then, as they realized that they had been deceived, their joy turned to anger and there was loud booing. Piles of newspapers announcing the victory were seized and burned on the boulevards.

The following morning, May 9th, there was the silence that follows all great catastrophes. There was no more anger now, no more indignation. Nungesser and Coli were officially reported missing, and the general stupefaction was giving way to sorrow and mourning; though many people still found it difficult to believe that the famous war ace Nungesser, whom no enemy had been able to destroy, should have disappeared without trace beneath the waters of the Atlantic. They still hoped against hope that he and his intrepid companion would turn up again somehow. There was no news of them? Very well, but that didn't mean they were lost. Very likely they had come down in the sea on account of engine trouble or something; there must still be a chance that they had been picked up by some small vessel without wireless. Such cases had been known—Hawker and Mackenzie Grieve, for example. Or they might have flown inland, driven from their course by bad weather, and been compelled to land in some out-of-the-way spot—in some Canadian forest perhaps, where they were miles from any house with a telephone. Moreover, Nungesser had put his name down not for the transatlantic flight Paris to New York, but for the long-distance record, which was something quite different. On arriving over the Atlantic at Newfoundland therefore he might have flown straight on instead of turning south to New York.

Hope springs eternal . . . And for many days it resulted in large numbers of optimistic but totally false reports. On May 24th a trawler was reported to have sighted a small cargo vessel towing a white hydroplane—that was obviously L'Oiseau Blanc; and hope bubbled up, soon to be dashed by an announcement of the British Admiralty that although the report was quite correct, the white-painted hydroplane was British. It had been forced down at sea and been taken in tow. . . . That was, of course, a disappointment, but at least it showed that there was still a chance.

Two other ships, the Dana and the Bellaline, both reported that they had sighted L'Oiseau Blanc not far from the American coast. Inquiries showed that both these ships were on the route *L'Oiseau Blanc* was to have followed, but at the time of the alleged sightings the machine could not possibly have been in the air any longer, because its fuel would long since have been exhausted.

'There's not much hope,' people began to admit, 'but couldn't the Canadians do something? After all, Nungesser and Coli might have come down there somewhere.' But what chance of success would even large-scale searches have in so enormous an area of forest and waste land? The whole frozen waste of Labrador, for example . . . And then came a report from Labrador from trappers, who declared that they had seen red rockets in the sky one evening at some distance from their camp. The next morning they went to the spot and investigated, but could find nothing. And after that there were one or two fantastic rumours, including the inevitable one that other trappers had seen two white men who were the prisoners of an Indian tribe.

People began to shrug their shoulders now. Nungesser and Coli . . . Those who had seen them off recalled every word and gesture; Coli's high spirits; his joke, the cod he was going to fish off Cape Cod. And they smiled; it was better than weeping. And still the fantastic reports came in. A Canadian trapper claimed to have found a document signed 'Nungesser' saying that he and Coli had come down in the Far North, and asking for help. This document was even sent to Paris. Madame Nungesser thought it was not unlike her son's handwriting, but on the other hand the text of the message made it seem impossible that the well-educated Nungesser could have written it.

Similar messages were found in bottles. Some of them turned up even years later: one in 1929 on the Dutch coast, another in 1933, and the last one in 1934. No doubt they were the work of the usual mentally unbalanced creatures who always do that sort of thing. But of real evidence as to the fate of the two intrepid airmen there was very little. How far had

they got? Some experts thought it possible that they had got
no farther than the Channel, where the weather they must have
run into was so bad that all air services and flights had been
suspended, and even ships had found themselves in difficulties.
As against this there was a fairly well authenticated report of a
sighting off the Irish coast at 10.05 hours on May 8th, which
meant that at least they had flown out over the Atlantic. Then
there were reports from Newfoundland that the noise of a
plane had been heard at a time when no other planes were
known to have been in the air in those parts. But the only
absolutely certain evidence was that of Captain Venson, one of
the flyers who accompanied *L'Oiseau Blanc* as far as the cliffs
of Étretat:

'She gradually vanished ahead of us in the opaque milky
haze tinged with red as day rose.'

5

Charles A. Lindbergh

'You understand we cannot let just anybody pilot our airplane across the ocean.'

The speaker was Charles A. Levine, President of the Columbia Aircraft Corporation. He was polite but very firm with his young visitor, who wanted to buy one of the Corporation's planes with the crack-brained idea of flying it from New York to Paris in one hop. The young fellow had given his name as Charles A. Lindbergh, but as far as the President of the Columbia Aircraft Corporation was concerned it might have been Charles A. anything. The young man said he was an air-mail pilot on the St. Louis to Chicago service.

The older man looked at him curiously. The lad looked even younger than he said he was, something like an overgrown schoolboy; and obviously he was still in the age when romantic dreams could easily be confused with hard fact. Between them on the big mahogany desk was a cheque for fifteen thousand dollars, the purchase price offered for the plane.

Money was money, of course, but the Columbia Aircraft Corporation was not short of it, and there was something else at stake: the Corporation's reputation. Of course, if by any chance the flight succeeded it would be a tremendous advertisement far outweighing monetary considerations. On the other hand, if it failed, and the odds were that it would fail, then with one of the Corporation's machines that wouldn't be so good.

'You should think it over,' advised Levine.

But Charles Lindbergh had already thought it over, and very carefully too. That money didn't belong to him. It had been raised by subscription amongst the citizens of St. Louis, who were supporting him in his plan to make the attempt, alone, on his own initiative, and at his own time. Lindbergh was anxious to secure the co-operation of the Columbia Aircraft Corporation, but he was not prepared to pay any price to obtain it. For example, he was not prepared to let anyone interfere with his own idea of how it ought to be done, and he was not prepared to have anyone else with him. The Columbia Aircraft Corporation wanted to take things into its own hands as the price of co-operation; in which case he and his fellow citizens would be paying 15,000 dollars for the pleasure of painting the name *Spirit of St. Louis* on the fuselage of one of the Corporation's planes. That would be a rather expensive pleasantry, young Lindbergh felt.

No, there was really nothing to think over; so he picked up his cheque, said good afternoon politely and left. It was February 1927 and it was muddy underfoot and there was a bitter wind. He didn't need Charles A. Levine to tell him that there were a good many people who regarded his undertaking as the overweening impertinence of a young fool who didn't know any better. It wasn't that they thought it impossible that one day the journey from New York to Paris would be carried out non-stop by air. It was just that they regarded the conditions in which he proposed to do it as fantastic: alone, and if possible in a single-engined plane. The main objection he had to listen to again and again, and one that was beginning to strain even his good temper, was that he would never be able to stay awake for the forty hours or so he would have to be in the air—if he succeeded.

'More than once in my life I have stayed awake for two days,' he would reply patiently.

'But not piloting a plane!'

'Yes, piloting a plane, and in difficult conditions too.'

That was at least one thing which could not be in doubt:

staying awake for the flight was just possible, though he was prepared to admit that there were certain dangers involved. On the other hand those dangers were well worth risking because he would save the weight of a fellow pilot or navigator, and thus be able to carry more fuel, which was the main consideration in such a flight. Further, the ability to decide rapidly, and even on the spur of the moment by sheer instinct, could be a matter of life or death on such a flight, and only a man on his own could react with such speed. If a second man were there sharing all the risks equally then any dangerous decision would first have to be discussed and an agreement come to. No, it was much better that there should be only one man—one man to take the risks, and one man to make the decisions.

'Why a single-engined plane?' they also wanted to know. 'Isn't that a very big risk to take?' One of the people who had asked that was the director of an aviation corporation. 'What percentage of engine-failures do you reckon with?' Lindbergh had riposted. It was quite clear, for example, that if you used a three-engined plane then, other things being equal, the likelihood of an engine defect was multiplied by three. And if one failed the two others would not be sufficient to take him over the Atlantic. Further, the more engines, the bigger and heavier the plane, and the greater weight of fuel it would have to carry. Take-off, heavily loaded with the great quantity of fuel necessary to carry it nearly 4,000 miles, would always be difficult—and dangerous, as the fatal mishap to René Fonck's Sikorski had shown in 1926. Moreover, there was the question of cost. For example an up-to-date Fokker of that type cost about 30,000 dollars, or twice as much as Lindbergh had available.

In view of all these things young Lindbergh found that what other people called his obstinate folly looked far more like firm reasonableness. But he'd have to find someone to agree with him soon because he needed a plane badly; within a matter of weeks if he were to be ready to take off with a fair chance against Byrd, Davis, Chamberlin, and those flyers over there in Europe who were proposing to make the flight in the east–west direction.

As far as his own qualifications for the job were concerned, young Lindbergh was quietly confident. He had been flying since his twenty-first birthday—not that that was so very long ago—when he had enrolled in a flying school in Nebraska. Since then he had flown in the air service of the War Department, receiving his commission as a flying officer. Since early in 1925 he had been flying regularly as an air-mail pilot on the St. Louis to Chicago route, and he had 2,000 flying hours to his credit—in all weathers and under all sorts of conditions: not a bad record for a youngster. Even so, when he thought of his rivals, mostly men with far greater experience, some of it during the war, men with far more powerful financial and other support behind them, he sometimes experienced a slight twinge of doubt. So far all he had behind him was the enthusiastic approval of a small group of friends in St. Louis, and that 15,000-dollar cheque. It wasn't a lot, but it ought to be enough —and the sooner he could turn that thin strip of paper into a plane the better!

Levine was not the only man young Lindbergh had approached without success. Some of the aircraft designers and constructors had politely refused; others had sought to impose conditions (as Levine had done); and the rest had been unable to provide him with anything suitable within the necessary time—or had asked too high a price. There was just one firm left: the Ryan Company at San Diego in California, a small firm building chiefly mail planes. Lindbergh went to San Diego and opened negotiations with them. Here he was lucky, and an agreement was quickly reached. For about 10,000 dollars the Ryan Company agreed to provide him with a machine according to his specifications, and this left him a fair margin for other expenses in connection with the flight.

'Phew!' he thought in relief as he left their offices after fixing things up. 'Little short of a miracle'! And he thought it a very good sign that the whole thing should begin with a miracle—enough people had already told him that if he succeeded it would only be by a miracle.

Almost every day after that he was in the works of the Ryan Company, discussing, supervising and watching the progress of the work. It was a rather out-of-date and rough-looking sort of place compared with the Columbia Aircraft Corporation's works, but as against that all the men in it were without exception enthusiastic and keen on their job; they worked devotedly on the small plane that was to be called the *Spirit of St. Louis*, and which would, they were all quite convinced, be the first machine to fly the Atlantic to Paris.

Another place he visited was the emporium of a ship's chandler on the quay, and from there he returned carrying a roll of something under his arm. When he spread it out on the desk it turned out to be a chart of the Atlantic Ocean. With his pencil he drew a line from New York to Paris and then looked at it raptly. After a while he followed that line carefully across the Atlantic, calculating the distances and the route until in his thoughts he was already a thousand, and then two thousand miles out into the Atlantic—which was more than half-way there. But supposing the one engine of his little plane gave out? It hardly bore thinking about, but it was a possibility; and Lindbergh decided that despite the weight he would have to take an inflatable rubber dinghy with him, signal rockets, and extra food and drink.

In the meantime the men at the Ryan Company worked like happy slaves to get his plane ready in time; the nearer they came to deadline the more impatient Lindbergh grew. On April 14th he learned that the French flyers Nungesser and Coli were carrying out their first trials with the machine they proposed to use on their flight. Byrd, Fonck and Davis were also reported to be practically ready and only waiting for favourable weather conditions, whilst Chamberlin had just broken the world record for a long-distance flight by staying in the air for over 51 hours. This latter news was a little disappointing for Lindbergh, who had hoped to set up a world record for flying duration himself before attempting to fly the Atlantic. Never mind, as yet no one had flown from New York to Paris—or the other way round. But time was growing short.

'How much longer will it be before she's ready?' he demanded.

'In a fortnight, Charlie,' came the reply. And that was the footing everyone was on in the Ryan Company; it was Charlie and Bill and Joe and Jack. If anything were wrong with that plane after all, it wouldn't be for lack of good will; the men were working night and day with enthusiasm, and they had identified themselves completely with Lindbergh's coming flight—with 'their' machine. And as for Lindbergh himself— well, he was 'Charlie' to them all.

On April 22nd the name of a new rival for transatlantic flying honours was announced: a Frenchman, Drouhin. The name of Costes was mentioned as another possibility. But as against the newcomer, an earlier and very formidable rival had faded out for the time being—Commander Byrd, whose machine had crashed on a test take-off. Of course, everyone wanted to be the first.

'Supposing one of the others manages it before you start, what will you do?' Lindbergh was asked.

'In that case I'll try something else,' he replied. 'Perhaps the Pacific, or a flight round the world. However, for the moment no one else has done it, and I shall go on preparing for it until someone else does succeed—and if no one has by the time I'm ready, I'll do it myself.'

In the meantime he tried to drive all thought of the others out of his mind, and to act as though he were the only one preparing to make the flight.

On April 26th he learned that Davis had been killed whilst making a test take-off with his plane *The American Legion*, and he felt more than ever convinced that his choice of a small plane was right. 'Those big planes are too heavy,' he thought. 'They're crashing one after the other.'

A couple of days later the *Spirit of St. Louis* was ready at last. Lindbergh looked at her with satisfaction, running his eye over her trim lines as she stood there waiting, fresh as a daisy in her silver-grey paint, with the name *Spirit of St. Louis* painted on her fuselage. He climbed into the cockpit and took off. She rose into the air without the slightest trouble, answered the controls sweetly, was fast, and proved very manageable. Just an adjustment or two here and there, and she would be perfect. In the following days he made further tests with heavier and heavier loads, and each time he was satisfied. She was ready, and so was he.

On May 8th he decided to take her to St. Louis, but before the take-off a friend arrived brandishing a newspaper.

'Nungesser and Coli have started, Charlie,' he exclaimed.

Lindbergh seized the paper and read the news. That was all, but it was enough. Lindbergh was thoughtful. It looked as though the French flyers had beaten him to it. Both were experienced war-time pilots.

'What are you going to do now, Charlie?'

'If they succeed—as they probably will—I'll change my objective. Fly over the Pacific instead.'

But before long he was thinking of the Atlantic again; Nungesser and Coli were missing, and whether they turned up again or not, they had failed to fly the Atlantic. He sincerely hoped that they would be saved, but it was too much to expect him to be sorry that they hadn't succeeded. The field was now free for his own attempt.

On May 10th he took off for St. Louis and arrived there at 14.25 hours. The following day he took off again, without attending the various functions in his honour; for one thing time was short, and for another he had done nothing to deserve them as yet. This time he landed on Curtis Airfield at 5.33 p.m., having set up a record for an overland flight—not a bad start. When he got out of his plane he was surrounded by newspapermen who bombarded him with questions. He answered mechanically, but then as he glanced up he spotted a three-engined Fokker coming in to land. It was his turn to ask questions now.

'Isn't that Byrd's plane?'

'Yes.'

'It's been repaired, then?'

'It's been ready for several days now.'

'And what about the *Bellanca*?' This was the Columbia Aircraft Corporation's plane.

'Lloyd Berthaud was going to fly it, but they've decided in favour of Chamberlin, and Berthaud's suing them for breach of contract.'

'Any news of Nungesser and Coli?'

'None, unfortunately.'

Lindbergh felt a surge of confidence sweep over him. He was ready, completely ready. All he needed now was a suitable weather forecast.

'It's not very favourable at the moment,' they told him. 'A trough of depression along the coast.'

The next day whilst Lindbergh was watching the mechanics overhaul the *Spirit of St. Louis*, a man came up and introduced himself. It was Commander Byrd.

'I thought I'd like to wish you good luck, Captain Lindbergh. By the way, you're welcome to use my arrangements at Roosevelt Field, and have my weather forecasts if you like.'

On May 16th the weather was so bad that a start was out of the question. That evening at Roosevelt Field he had a talk with Kimball, the chief of the meteorological service.

'Obviously, if you're not going to follow the shipping routes that makes it more difficult for us to forecast the weather you are likely to encounter, because we just don't know exactly what's happening in more northern latitudes.'

All the same, Kimball thought Lindbergh could rely on an improvement in the weather for the following day. But on May 19th there was fine steady rain, and the tops of the skyscrapers were hardly visible in the mist.

D

'Let's go to the theatre tonight, Charlie. It'll take you mind off things,' suggested a friend.

'We might as well, I suppose. There's nothing to be done in weather like this.'

A few hours later though, he asked someone to ring up Kimball for him—just in case.

'Well?' demanded Lindbergh when the friend returned.

'There's been a sudden and unexpected improvement in the weather, but it's still far from ideal. In a day or so it ought to be all right . . .'

'To hell with that!' exclaimed Lindbergh excitedly. 'I'm off to Roosevelt Field. I shall leave at dawn.'

After making the necessary arrangements at the airfield he returned to his hotel to try and get some sleep, but he didn't succeed; his mind was too busy. Was he right to chance it? Would he manage even the take-off? Look what had happened to Fonck's Sikorski, and to Davis, and the *America*! Everything ruined before they could even start. And after such hard work and such high hopes! On the other hand Chamberlin had managed the take-off with his plane, and he had beaten the world's long distance record. And at least Nungesser and Coli had been able to take-off. How far had they got after all, and where were they now? Drifting on the Atlantic with their plane? Or lost in some Canadian forest? Or dead; drowned in the sea or killed in a crash?

There was a knock at the door. Lindbergh started up; he found it hard to realize that it was time to get up—he hadn't slept a wink.

When he left the hotel to go to the airfield he looked up. It was still dark, but there wasn't a star to be seen, and New York was shrouded in mist. When he arrived at Roosevelt Field his plane had been wheeled out on to the runway and everything was ready for the take-off. Lindbergh thought over the situation rapidly. The airfield was bare, wet and misty. Beyond it at the other end of the runway lay the Atlantic; and beyond that, a very, very long way beyond that, was Europe—and Paris, his objective.

A little group of mechanics and airfield personnel stood by and looked at the young man curiously. Standing on his own in the early morning twilight he looked slimmer and younger than ever, and far from tough. You could tell nothing from his face, but he would probably have to call the flight off again. The ground was sodden and heavy, and that would make the take-off more difficult; there was a bank of cloud ahead, and altogether these were quite enough reasons to justify a postponement. Then Lindbergh would return to his hotel for breakfast, and listen to his friends assuring him how wise he had been.

Suddenly Lindbergh felt a great urge to go, to take his chance. He felt he just couldn't turn back again; he climbed into the cockpit of the *Spirit of St. Louis* and settled himself into the cane seat at the controls. That bank of cloud and fog was still ahead, a very graphic symbol of the unknown dangers he proposed to challenge. There was a high wind, too; he could feel it making the wings vibrate as he sat there in the enclosed cockpit. There was still time to abandon the flight; not a soul would dream of reproaching him. But resolutely he gave the signal the mechanics were waiting for but not expecting, and they removed the chocks. Lindbergh made contact, the propeller began to swing and the engine to roar, and then the *Spirit of St. Louis* started to move, slowly at first, and then more and more quickly.

Swathes of water fountained into the air, swished up by the plane's wheels as it rolled more and more swiftly along the sodden runway. Half-way along, the tail wheel lifted from the ground and then dropped back again. Inside the cockpit Lindbergh was jubilant; he was quite sure that he was going to get the two and a half tons off the ground safely. His eyes were on the long lines of telegraph wires at the end of the runway. They represented the first obstacle he had to surmount. With his hands on the controls he tried again, and obediently the tail rose, but he made no attempt to get into the air; he wanted to take advantage of his increasing speed. Another couple of hundred yards or so, and then . . . This time it was now or never. The *Spirit of St. Louis* rose into the air lightly as though the glue-like surface had no power to hold her. Lindbergh had done it! The first big difficulty had been surmounted. He was in the air!

He was flying about fifty feet above sea level, and ahead of him he could see the flat bluish mass of Cape Cod. Before long there would be nothing but the endless stretch of the Atlantic around him, with nothing but water as far as eye could see. Now, perhaps for the first time, he realized the full audacity of his flight and the dangers he would have to surmount if he were going to be successful. 'The Flying Fool' the newspapers had called him; perhaps they were right after all. Below him that vast stretch of greenish, greyish sea flecked with foam was probably the grave of Nungesser and Coli, two brave men who had attempted to do what he was now attempting to do. He nosed down closer to the low, rolling waves, coming down to meet the ocean 'asking its favour—the right to pass for thousands of miles across its realm.' as he wrote later on in his book *The Spirit of St. Louis*. The window of the cockpit was open to one side, and he leant out and looked down. A fresh breeze blew in his face and into the cockpit, lifting the chart he had been studying and carrying it towards the open window as the breeze swept into the cabin and out again.

Concentrating on piloting the plane, Lindbergh did not notice at first what was happening, but the chart was flapping in the wind now and moving still nearer to the opening. If he lost it that would be the end of his flight; the *Spirit of St. Louis* would be flying blind, with little hope of ever reaching Europe. It was that chart which showed him the magic contours of the objective he was aiming it. Without it he would be helpless. And then suddenly Lindbergh heard the flapping— not a moment too soon. He turned his head to the left and saw his precious chart about to disappear for good and all out of the open window. There was no time for thought, his hand shot out instinctively—and just caught hold of the chart and retrieved it in the nick of time. He took a deep breath which was more like a sigh. That was a narrow escape! Carefully he folded up the chart and put it into a place of safety.

What a ridiculous end that would have been to a high endeavour! If he had had to return to Roosevelt Field they would have bombarded him with questions. 'What happened? Feed-pipe broken? Fuel leak?' And what would he have had to reply? 'No, I just lost my chart.' He shivered at the thought. If there's one thing a young man finds it difficult to stand it's ridicule. And that situation would have been truly ridiculous— even if no one had said a further word. Their silence would have been even worse. 'What an idiot!' they would be thinking. 'Fly the Atlantic? Why, he couldn't even take care of his chart!'

He smiled in relief at his escape. He was over Nova Scotia now, but a great bank of thick cloud barring his way was hardly comforting. The wind was rising too, and the *Spirit of St. Louis* was shuddering and creaking in the sudden squalls that buffeted her. Bursts of rain swept over her wings and spattered the glass of the cockpit. It was probably only a local disturbance, but it might well prove decisive, because unless he could identify the exact point at which he left the mainland behind it would throw out his whole flight across the Atlantic.

Then the rain gave way to mist. 'Let's hope it will clear up before I get to Cape Breton,' he thought anxiously, and his mind now began to turn on other difficulties. He had no sextant, no parachute—'What good would a parachute be to me over the sea?' he had wanted to know—and no wireless. He was certainly alone now, in every sense of the word. Supposing the coasts of Europe were covered in mist and fog, too? He tried to dismiss such disagreeable thoughts. Sufficient for the day . . . In any case the visibility was already improving: he could see the ocean and the long coastline, and was able to correct his course slightly. He could see icebergs floating below him now; it was as though he were flying back into the winter and leaving the spring behind.

Newfoundland must loom ahead shortly. It was the point from which all those who had attempted the Atlantic flight before him had left the New World behind. Lieut.-Comdr. Read's heavy U.S. Navy hydroplanes on their way to England via the Azores; the near miss of Hawker and Mackenzie Grieve with their Sopwith biplane; the converted Vickers-Vimy bomber of Alcock and Brown on the first successful non-stop transatlantic flight eight years before. And now here he was, the first man to fly alone, and follow in their footsteps—and attempt to fly even farther, not to the first point of land on the way, Ireland, but on to Paris—from New York!

There was still land below him, violet and peaceful in the twilight, the smoke rising gently from the chimneys of farms. But ahead of him was the mighty ocean and the blackness of night, the unknown into which he was now to plunge.

The sea below him was dotted with icebergs floating along like sea-monsters and showing up very white against the dark sea. Lindbergh had decided to take the shortest route, and that was clearly a segment of the great circle. But at the same time it was the loneliest route, because at that time of the year shipping took the more southerly route, due to the presence of those floating icebergs below him. Lindbergh remembered the fate of the White Star liner *Titanic*, the biggest ship in the world at the time. She had collided with an iceberg on her maiden voyage with over two thousand people on board, and more than fifteen hundred of them had been drowned in those icy seas. Though only a schoolboy at that time—it had been 1912—Lindbergh had read all about it. 'I shouldn't be much better off myself if I had to go down amongst that lot,' he thought. He shrugged his shoulders. Much better to remind himself that a third of his journey was already behind him; that he had plenty of fuel left to fly the rest; that so far he had kept his course accurately; and that there was a tail wind helping him on the way.

For the moment there seemed little to worry about as far as the elements were concerned, but precisely on that account a new danger was now threatening—Lindbergh was feeling tired, and that was the one thing he must not give way to. If he feel asleep, even if he only nodded off for a moment, he might find himself plunging into the sea. The first time he had felt tired he had easily succeeded in conquering the feeling, but then he had been aided by the fact that it was still light, and he had had to keep his wits about him because a series of troubles faced him. But now it was dark, and everything was going smoothly.

'The cold will help me to keep awake,' he thought, and he went up to ten thousand feet and flew at that height for a while. He was right; it was very cold, and the low temperature banished all desire to nod off. He looked out keenly. It was dark, but away to the east there was a faint light; the moon was about to rise. He searched the sky for familiar constellations, and then something about the look of his wings attracted his attention. There was an unusual metallic shine on them, and suddenly he realized that it was ice. Up there in the cold ice had formed on his wings. Icing, the deadly danger to a plane, threatening to make it heavier, to upset its trim, and lower its speed. He went down to lower altitudes so that the warmer air could dispose of the ice before the icing reached danger point. And as for the threat of falling asleep, he would have to combat it in some other way.

It was there though all the time, insidious and dangerous, ready to overwhelm the lonely man the moment he let himself go. Fortunately the moon was rising, and its gentle light bathed the clouds and created an unnatural world around him. Resolutely, Lindbergh made up his log. He had been sixteen hours in the air already and he had covered 1,600 miles, leaving him with just about 2,000 miles still to do. His engine was running sweetly, the plane was keeping on her course well, and everything was in order. The only danger at the moment was the old invisible enemy—sleep. And how good it would be just to doze off, if only for a few moments! But that was the one thing above all else he must not do—not even close his eyes for a couple of seconds. If he did he might never open them again in safety.

'In an hour the sun will be up,' he thought. 'And thank goodness for that. Everything will be easier then.'

The fight to remain awake went on. Sometimes it almost seemed to him that his soul had left his body, that it was wandering down the pleasant lanes of the past, back even to his childhood. Faces he had not seen for years came into his mind, incidents from his life as an air-mail pilot. And it all seemed very far away, like something in a dream.

Had he dozed off? Yes, it seemed that despite his determination he had, for he found himself using the controls, putting the plane back on her course, setting her on an even keel again. He gritted his teeth. 'Keep awake, man!' he muttered to himself. 'Keep awake whatever you do!' But sleep was surrounding his body in a mist far more dangerous than that which surrounded his machine. That mist might reduce visibility, but it did not stop the engine. But this other mist threatened to destroy everything. Now and again he found himself keeping his eyelids open with his fingers. All his hopes were fixed on daylight now, as though that would be the end of his troubles. Well, at least the daylight would help him in the struggle to keep awake.

He stared eagerly towards the east, seeking for the lightening in the clouds that would tell him dawn was on the way. He was about half-way now: 1,800 miles behind him; another 1,800 miles ahead of him. And there at last was the first unmistakable sign of dawn. Before long it spread over the whole sky. It was a strange, almost solid dawn, as though it were thick. Then he realized that there was a special reason—a thick mist.

He frowned. Mist was the one real physical danger that threatened him now. He had seen what it meant over Nova

Scotia. If it were as misty when he reached Europe he might lose his way. He took his plane down to see whether it were still misty at a lower altitude. It was just as bad at 2,000 feet, but a little lower than that he caught sight of the sea, and breathed a sigh of relief. There were sea-horses in plenty and their heads pointed north-west. The wind was behind him and helping him on his way to Europe—and by the time he got there the mist might have cleared away.

The sun rose and soon it was broad daylight. Before long he had been twenty-four hours, a whole day and a night in the air. He was certainly tired, but the danger of sleep was not so great now, because there was much more to take his attention: the sea, for example. Carefully he searched the endless surface in the hope of spotting a ship. He went lower, for he thought he had noticed some islands, but he could find nothing. Then he made out a black point and went still lower to examine it more closely. It was a porpoise, the first living thing he had seen in twenty-four hours. An hour later he spotted further black points; first one and then another. This time, however, he knew from his height that they could not be porpoises. He went down lower to see them better, and found that they were trawlers.

He throttled back his engine and soared low over them. There was not a sign of life on board any of them. Then a porthole opened and he saw a face staring up at him. He shouted and waved, but there was no response, and in a moment he was past and wondering whether the whole thing had been a hallucination. But there was no time to turn back and make sure; if he kept on his course he could hope to spot land in about three hours. If his calculations were correct . . . But were they? And had he really kept so strictly to his course as he reckoned? At least those trawlers seemed to indicate that land was not so very far away.

Stretching across the horizon to the north-west was a long line of cloud, serrated and irregular, almost like the first sight of a rocky coast. As he came nearer the illusion became stronger until finally there was no possibility of doubt; he realized excitedly that he was looking at a coastline, and that the green behind it was cultivated land—and, yes, there were roads running through it.

'It must be Ireland,' he thought. 'Two and a half hours ahead of schedule.' It was this which exercised his mind at first even more than the thought that he had flown the Atlantic. It was no mirage, or if it were then it was a mirage of other senses besides sight, for he could whiff the sweeter, softer smell of land, of rich humus, above the smell of the sea.

He took the *Spirit of St. Louis* down in a spiral descent to see if he could discover any human beings on that lovely island. Yes, there they were; moving figures looking up at him. As he flew on he could see more land in the distance, another coast line, while in between were the waters of St. George's Channel, with ships sailing through it as though on a river. That other land was England. Still farther on was the mainland of Europe waiting to welcome him, the first man to fly direct to it from America. His journey was not over yet: Paris was about 600 miles ahead, but his engine was running as sweetly as ever, and he had little doubt of complete victory now.

'I've got enough fuel left to go on to Rome if I felt inclined,' he thought. 'But no, Paris is my objective.'

But a little while after that it began to look as though he wouldn't be able to get even as far as Paris. The engine, which had served him so well throughout the long flight over the Atlantic, began to cough, splutter and miss, making the whole plane shudder. Lindbergh anxiously took his plane down, but this time he was looking for somewhere to land. It was his instinctive reaction: get down safely. Then he had a closer look at his instrument panel. The oil flow was normal, but the pressure was down to zero. So that was the cause of the trouble! He opened the reserve tank and listened anxiously: at first there was no change, and the engine continued to splutter and miss, but then, after what seemed a very long time, but could have been only a very short one, the engine

(*Right*) Walter Wellman,
the first man to attempt
a transatlantic flight.

(*Below*) The dirigible *America*, in which Wellman and his crew made their
unsuccessful attempt.

(*Above*) The U.S. Navy Curtiss hydroplane NC-4, the first heavier-than-air machine to fly the Atlantic—by stages via the Azores.

(*Left*) The cockpit of the NC-4, showing the instrument panel.
(*Photo: Keystone*)

(*Above*) The Sopwith biplane in which the British airmen Hawker and Mackenzie Grieve made the first attempt to fly the Atlantic non-stop in a heavier-than-air machine.

(*Below*) The first men to fly the Atlantic non-stop in a heavier-than-air machine: the British airmen Lieutenant Arthur W. Brown and Captain John Alcock.
(*Photo: Keystone*)

(*Above*) Franco's hydroplane, the *Plus Ultra*, crossing Pernambuco harbour after its successful transatlantic flight.

(*Below*) The British dirigible R-34, the first airship to make the non-stop transatlantic crossing in either direction. (*Photo: Keystone*)

(*Right*) The French airmen, Nungesser and Coli, in their plane *L'Oiseau Blanc* before attempting the first non-stop east–west Atlantic crossing by heavier-than-air machine. (*Photo: Monde et Caméra*)

(*Left*) René Cousinet (left), the designer of the *Arc-en-Ciel* (in background), in which Jean Mermoz (right) flew from France to South America non-stop. (*Photo: Collection Cos sira*)

(*Left*) Charles A. Lindbergh, the first man to fly the Atlantic solo and non-stop.

(*Below*) Lindbergh coming in to land at Croydon from Paris after his Atlantic flight.
(*Photos: Keystone*)

(*Above*) Levine and Chamberlin in the plane in which they flew the Atlantic non-stop from New York to Germany. (*Photo: Monde et Caméra*)

(*Left*) Lloyd Bertaud, who was to have piloted Levine's machine, but who, like so many others, quarrelled with him.

(*Above, left*) Captain George Haldeman, who piloted Ruth Elder's plane on an attempt to fly from New York to Paris. They came down in the sea off the Azores. (*Right*) Ruth Elder, the "American Girl", giving autographs at Le Bourget after her unsuccessful transatlantic attempt.

(*Below*) The Junkers plane *Bremen* sets off for Ireland to make its east–west attempt to cross the Atlantic.

(*Above*) Hermann Köhl, Major Fitzmaurice and Baron von Huenefeld, the first men to make the non-stop east–west crossing in a heavier-than-air machine.

(*Below*) The *Bremen* coming in to land.   (*Photos: Keystone*)

(*Above*) The French airmen Lotti, Lefèvre and Assolant, who flew the Atlantic from west to east and made a forced landing in Spain. On their left is the American, Schreiber. (*Photo: Monde et Caméra*)

(*Below*) The Australian airman Kingsford-Smith and his plane, the *Southern Cross*, at Heston aerodrome before he left on his record flight to Australia.

(*Above*) The French airmen Costes and Bellonte, who made the first non-stop transatlantic flight from Paris to New York, about to set off on a record-breaking long-distance overland flight in their plane, the *Point d'Interrogation*.

Costes

Bellonte
(*Photos: Collection Cossira*)

(*Above*) The American airwoman Amelia Earhart after her successful solo non-stop transatlantic flight. (*Photo: Keystone*)

(*Below*) The German dirigible *Graf Zeppelin* at Lakehurst in the United States after her first transatlantic flight. (*Photo: The Mansell Collection*)

settled down to its old smooth running, and the vibration ceased. Once again Lindbergh heaved a tremendous sigh of relief.

He was flying along the Channel now; that was Plymouth to the left, and that black line along the horizon to the right was France. His approach had been noticed and reported now, and by the time he reached the estuary of the Seine and turned inland to Paris, the streets and roads leading to Le Bourget were crowded with cars and people making their way there to welcome him when he touched down—to welcome him with the same enthusiasm they would have shown for Nungesser and Coli on their return if they had succeeded.

Yet Lindbergh had not been at all sure that he would be received with enthusiasm. Those who thought they knew had advised him to postpone his attempt for a while, declaring that the French would not welcome the success of an American so soon after the failure and loss of their own men. Fortunately Lindbergh had refused to let that affect his decision. There were great dangers in the flight, and men of flesh and blood had to meet and surmount them—irrespective of their nationality.

As he flew over France now and came closer and closer to his objective Lindbergh felt deeply moved, and he was struck by the neatness and cleanliness of the countryside; in fact it impressed him so much that instead of throwing out of the window the paper bag in which his sandwiches had been wrapped, he put it into his pocket until he could find a waste-paper basket. He wasn't going to do anything to disturb that enormous neatness and tidiness! It was rapidly growing dark now, and lights were beginning to spring up below him. Then in the distance he saw a big light flash regularly: the searchlight on the Eiffel Tower. It was Paris! And although it was evening, that welcoming light was very much like the dawn of a new day in aviation—the Atlantic had been fully conquered at last.

6

Chamberlin and Levine

A<small>T</small> 15.00 hours on June 5th, 1927, an officer of the U.S. cruiser *Memphis*, which had just left Cherbourg on her way to New York, knocked at the door of a cabin occupied by a young man in civilian clothing.

'I though this wireless message might interest you,' said the officer as he came into the cabin. 'We've just received it from the *Mauretania*, which is about twelve miles off at the moment.'

The young man read the wireless message, and then asked: 'We're about three hundred miles from the Irish coast now, aren't we?'

'Three hundred and forty, to be precise.'

'Which means that they're quite certain to succeed, and there's no one who hopes more sincerely than I do that they will land safely.'

That young man was more capable of expressing an authoritative opinion than most, for his name was Charles A. Lindbergh, and he was now returning to the United States after his successful transatlantic flight. The message from the *Mauretania* was to the effect that *Miss Columbia* the plane being flown across the Atlantic by Clarence Chamberlin and Charles A. Levine and which had taken off from New York at dawn on June 4th, had just flown over the great liner.

Charles A. Levine? Lindbergh smiled to himself, and he recalled their meeting and Levine's discouraging words: 'You understand we cannot let just anybody pilot our airplane across the ocean.' He remembered Levine's polite but rather distant attitude ensconced there behind his great mahogany desk. Levine himself was now facing the fatigues and dangers of a transatlantic air crossing, and there was no one better able to appreciate what that meant than young Lindbergh. That interview lay four months back, and quite a lot had happened since then. Charles A. Lindbergh was no longer 'just anybody', but a famous young man who had inscribed his name for all time in the history of aviation.

By this time Levine must be feeling a good deal of mortification at his lack of confidence in the youngster who had come to him for help. And the interesting thing was that Charles A. Levine was now flying the Atlantic under much the same conditions—in a one-engined machine. Another man, Clarence Chamberlin, was piloting his plane, and Levine himself was merely a passenger.

Right up to the night of June 3rd it was not generally known who was going to fly with Chamberlin. 'You will learn in good time,' Levine had said in reply to eager questioning. In consequence there was a good deal of speculation as to the name of the second member of the crew: Berthaud? Acosta?

There was another question which greatly interested everyone, and, above all, of course, the journalists: Where would the plane, *Miss Columbia*, make for? 'We shall try to beat Lindbergh's record,' was all Chamberlin would say. And from this it was assumed that he would try to fly on farther than Paris, perhaps to Berlin, or Rome. Perhaps even to Moscow?

In the early morning of June 4th *Miss Columbia* stood on the runway ready to take off. Chamberlin was waiting there, of course, but there was no other likely man to go with him. Charles A. Levine was there, in his capacity as President of the Columbia Aircraft Corporation, accompanied by his wife, to see Chamberlin off. It began to look as though Chamberlin were going to make a solo flight over the Atlantic as Lindbergh had just done. He was in the cockpit now, and everything was ready. The propeller began to turn. The cockpit door was still open and Levine reached up to it, apparently to close it, but with a smile and a wave to his astonished wife he climbed into the cockpit instead and closed the door after him. Immediately *Miss Columbia* began to move along the runway, rapidly gathering speed for the take-off.

Everything had happened so swiftly and so unexpectedly that for a moment everyone was flabbergasted. Mrs. Levine had gone white. Her husband had not even told her of his intention to go with Chamberlin.

'It's all right,' said a voice at her elbow, 'they're just making a trial run together.'

And so it seemed, for with relief Mrs. Levine saw that the plane had slowed down and turned round, and was now returning to the point it had started from. John Carisi, the chief engineeer of the Columbia Air Corporation, who had been responsible for the preparations, went up to the plane, opened the cockpit door and spoke to Levine.

'What are you up to, Mr. Levine? I must say you gave us all a shock. Your wife's quite upset; she thought you were going to fly to Europe.'

Levine smiled, but said nothing, and closed the cockpit door again. Once more *Miss Columbia* started her run. This time she did not slow down, but gathering speed she rose into the air and disappeared in the direction of the Atlantic. This time Mrs. Levine sank back into a faint, supported by sympathetic arms. For a while the others stood there hardly saying a word. They still weren't sure what was happening, and they thought that perhaps *Miss Columbia* would come into sight again and land. But the sound of her engine had already died away, and another attempt to cross the Atlantic in a non-stop flight was in progress.

When *Miss Columbia* flew over the *Mauretania* only a few hundred miles from the Irish coast it was generally assumed that the flight would be successful, since by far the greater part of the journey was already behind the flyers. But towards evening, when nothing further was heard, doubts began to arise. By this time the waters of the Channel were being whipped up by a gusty west wind; Belgium and the Nether-lands were enveloped in fog; and no one knew just where Chamberlin's plane was or where it was making for. As dark-ness fell on June 5th, airfield runway lights were on in all the big towns that seemed likely objectives: Paris, Brussels, Amsterdam, Berlin . . . Where were Chamberlin and Levine making for? Signal rockets went into the air at intervals and searchlights picked their way across the clouds, but there was no sign of the plane.

No further news of the *Miss Columbia* had been heard since she was sighted over Plymouth at 21.15 hours. In Berlin they reckoned with a landing at about three o'clock in the morning, if Berlin were the objective—and if all went well. In fact, at that moment the two Americans were doing their best to find some landmark to give them their position. They just weren't sure where they were. Then Levine drew his pilot's attention to an intermittent glow to the right of their plane. The clouds there lighted up red; then the glow faded for a moment or two, to return again. Chamberlin watched the phenomenon with interest.

'But for the colour I would have said it's the reflection of some sort of searchlight on the clouds, but it doesn't look like electric light. Let's go down and see.'

He took the plane down in a long spiral, and as they emerged from the cloud cover at a lower altitude they could see that the reflection came from a great fire. Flames were rising and then being beaten down and spread over the ground by gusts of wind. At first they thought it was a conflagration, but then they noticed that at a little distance there was another source of similar flames. According to Chamberlin's calculation they ought to be over Germany, the big industrial belt along the Ruhr.

'They're blast-furnaces,' he said suddenly.

'But where?' queried Levine.

They studied the map. It was beginning to get lighter now, and they could make out industrial installations, factory chimneys, and many railway lines and sidings. Then a few miles to the south they saw a signal rocket mount into the sky and burst.

'That's for us,' said Chamberlin. 'They're on the lookout for us,' and he turned the plane towards the place from which the rocket had been fired. A couple of minutes later the strained look left his face. 'Look down there,' he said. Below them was unmistakably an airfield, with hangars and runways.

Chamberlin took the plane down towards a group of men they could see on the airfield. As he approached they dispersed in all directions, obviously thinking that he intended to land, but, leaning out of the cockpit he shouted: 'Berlin? Berlin?'

And at that a number of men pointed towards the north-east.

'Do you think they understood me?' asked Levine as Chamberlin took the plane up again. 'According to this map Berlin ought to be to the east.'

'Ought to be . . . That is if we're where we thought we were. Perhaps we aren't. If they really did understand us then we must be farther south than we thought. I think the best thing we can do is to follow the direction they indicated.'

There was a moment's silence. 'Of course, we could try to land hereabouts somewhere.' he added. The petrol gauge showed about ten gallons left in the tank.

'Try to get to Berlin,' Levine decided.

'I'm not sure there's enough fuel left for that,' Chamberlin said, 'particularly as I don't know how far it is.'

In fact the industrial town over which they had just flown was Dortmund, and they were much farther south than their calculations had suggested. Berlin was 250 miles away—to the north-east, as the men on the aerodrome at Dortmund had indicated. A little before six o'clock in the morning the engine began to miss, a sure sign that before long it would stop. No town of any kind was in sight, and beneath the plane as it began to lose height was a great forest of what looked like pine trees. Chamberlin was beginning to get alarmed when he caught sight of grassland.

'We're light now,' he said; 'we shan't be risking too much, but we've just got to land.'

Within a very short space of time he had put the plane down safely not far from a group of peasants at work in the fields. With stiff and aching limbs the two Americans got out of their plane and eagerly sniffed the rich smell of the soil that was being turned over. Birds were singing joyfully in the trees as though to welcome them back to earth. Peasants were surrounding them and their machine with voluble interest, but it was not easy to make themselves understood. At last they grasped that it was petrol the airmen needed. Whether they really understood that the two men had flown from New York was another matter. However, petrol, it appeared, could be obtained from a nearby village. It was a long time before it arrived, and when it did it was in a horse-drawn cart, and there was about twenty-two gallons of it.

'Something like a hundred miles to go,' said Chamberlin. 'We ought to be able to do it—just about. We'll try, anyway.'

Then they tried to discover the exact direction from the peasants, but opinions differed. Finally when they had tanked up they took off in the direction indicated by the majority. But no big town came into sight.

'You were wrong to listen to them,' said Levine. 'Turn more northwards.'

'I'm piloting this plane,' said Chamberlin shortly.

Nerves were on edge now, and the discussion became sharp. At one point Levine even seized the controls, and Chamberlin gave way, but then he insisted on following his own instinct. In the end their fuel tank was practically empty and the engine began to miss again.

'Nothing left?' demanded Levine.

'Nothing,' replied Chamberlin. 'We shall have to land again.'

It was eleven o'clock now, and Chamberlin found a suitable spot and took *Miss Columbia* down. He was not so successful with his forced landing this time. *Miss Columbia* touched down, rolled along heavily, and then tipped her nose forward, smashing the propeller against the ground.

'That's it,' said Chamberlin. 'We're grounded now all right.'

The two men were depressed. Their transatlantic flight had succeeded splendidly—and then at the last moment they had to lose their way. Chamberlin pushed aside an old peasant woman who had come up shouting excitedly. She seemed to be demanding compensation for the damage *Miss Columbia* had done to her improvised landing field.

It appeared that they were near Cottbus, a town of some fifty thousand inhabitants about sixty miles south-south-east of Berlin. So near and yet so far . . .

The local mayor received them warmly and got into touch on their behalf with the Berlin airfield at Tempelhof, and a new propeller was sent post-haste by lorry. *Miss Columbia* took the air again and touched down in the German capital on June 7th. Chamberlin and Levine had flown non-stop from New York to the village of Bischofsrode, a distance of about 3,900 miles, in a flight of 42 hours. They had broken Lindbergh's non-stop long-distance record by about 300 miles.

7

Commander Richard Byrd

AT dawn on July 1st, 1927, the keeper of the small lighthouse
at Ver-sur-Mer in the Calvados area woke up with a start,
under the impression that someone was knocking at his door.
He listened. At first all he could hear was the soughing of the
sea, which had been enveloped in heavy mist all night. There
was no sound from the nearby village. From the road, however,
he could hear footsteps—those of fishermen, no doubt. 'Must
have been dreaming,' he muttered, and he turned over and
went to sleep again.

But a few minutes previously a man on a bicycle had been
steering his way between the puddles on the muddy road, his
carbide lamp throwing a yellow halo ahead of him, when
suddenly he had been forced to brake so hard that he nearly
fell off his machine. Two shadowy figures had loomed up
before him, and one of them was waving his arms to bring him
to a halt, which he had certainly succeeded in doing. The other
man—they were both big fellows—stood a little to one side.
They were shouting something the cyclist couldn't understand, and he assumed that they were drunk and playing some
damned silly trick, so suddenly he pedalled on again and
escaped them, though they almost succeeded in grabbing his
luggage carrier as he passed.

A quarter of an hour later the proprietor of a local hotel was
woken up by knocking on his door. He at least was in no
doubt about it, being, of course, more used to such a happening. He leant out of the window and saw two men standing in
the street below him gesticulating. And he too thought he had

to do with a couple of drunks—at that hour of the morning!
'Go and sleep off your hang-over somewhere else,' he shouted
with determination, after which he slammed the window and
went back to bed.

He wasn't the last man to woken up in the village that night.
There was Coeffier, for example, the Mayor's right hand. But
he knew the two men who knocked him up. They were local
fishermen, Martin and Marius.

'We've just seen a couple of odd folk,' they informed him.
'They were dripping wet, and they seemed to be English. Do
you think they could be shipwrecked mariners?'

Actually there turned out to be four of them disturbing the
peace of the little French fishing village that night. Their names
were Byrd, Noville, Acosta and Balchen, and they had just
made the fourth successful crossing of the Atlantic by aeroplane
—though not without difficulty.

Commander Byrd was delighted when he heard of Lindbergh's success. In any case, his own plan was somewhat
different, and Lindbergh's success did not affect it. Lindbergh
had become the first man to fly the Atlantic both non-stop and
solo. A splendid achievement, but it was not quite what Byrd
was after. He was thinking of the future—and airmen would
not be flying solo then, but with big planes carrying scores of
passengers regularly and safely to Europe and back. Byrd was
anxious to study the conditions in which such a regular transport service could be started, which was something very
different from Lindbergh's great adventure. Byrd proposed to
use a big three-engined plane, the *America*, equipped with
wireless and the latest navigational and flying instruments.
Moreover, he was not out to break any records either for speed
or distance. What he wanted to do was to make a crossing
which would pave the way for the regular commercial
passenger crossings of the future. What his flight actually did
was to high-light all the dangers still involved in transatlantic
flying.

Byrd and his crew took off from New York at dawn on June 29th, 1927, after having waited five days for favourable weather conditions. Five days earlier, on June 24th, the *America* had trundled along the runway, but without a crew and without her engines running. She had been carried away by a violent storm, and from all sides excited mechanics and ground personnel came rushing to save her, which, with a great deal of hard work and no little risk, they did, getting her safely away into a hangar. By great good luck, the damage the plane had suffered in the storm proved easily repairable.

More than one pessimist said that it was a bad omen for the coming flight, and that the plane would become the sport of the storms over the Atlantic. Byrd heard it and shrugged his shoulders. He was not superstitious. He believed that man could master his own fate, and as far as his transatlantic flight was concerned he had left nothing to chance: every precaution had been taken and every possible preparation most carefully made. Storms, high winds, cloud and mist had all been taken into consideration and provided against. In fact, Byrd rather hoped that the flight would prove difficult, for that was the only way in which it could provide him with valuable lessons.

For the moment his chief worry was whether they would succeed in getting the heavily-laden machine off the ground safely. Even the full power of its three large engines would not be too much to lift eight tons off the ground. To help the take-off he had decided to start her from an inclined runway. In this way he hoped that she would gain extra momentum for the take-off.

At dawn on June 29th the *America* was perched on the inclined plane which Byrd had had built, and the four men who were to fly in her were putting on their flying helmets and enjoying a last cigarette. Byrd himself climbed into the enclosed cabin first to check the controls, but when the others clambered in after him he gave up the pilot's seat to Balchen. The engines were started up, and before long they were racing at full throttle.

Behind the *America* stood a man with an axe. At a signal it would be his job to sever the rope which kept the *America* on the inclined take-off. Byrd gave the signal; a mechanic in full sight both of Byrd and the man with the axe passed it on, the axe swung down, and amidst the roar of the engines the rope was cut neatly in two and the big machine rolled forward, leaving the planks in a chaotic heap behind, and moving swiftly along the runway. Byrd's calculations proved correct. After running between five and six hundred yards the tail of the *America* rose for the first time, and then at something over twelve hundred yards the great plane rose slowly and heavily into the air.

Cheering began, but died away almost immediately. The *America* was in the air, but she was not gaining height; in fact she had definitely lost altitude, and her nose had turned down. For two or three seconds the watchers stood there with their hearts in their mouths—and then the *America* lifted her nose again, gaining height until she rose away out of danger.

'That was one hell of a take-off!'

The four men in the enclosed cabin were smiling now, but it certainly had been one hell of a take-off. Twenty minutes had passed since the first few anguishing minutes before it finally became clear that they were going to become airborne safely. The *America* had sufficient altitude now, and no difficulty in maintaining it. Her course was set for Newfoundland. What those who had been anxiously watching the take-off did not know was that Balchen had deliberately put down the nose of the *America* at Byrd's instructions. It was a dangerous man-œuvre, but it did give them that little extra speed which then enabled them to rise more easily.

Towards midday Byrd saw the sprawling town of Halifax coming into view. To the north the sun appeared through the clouds at last, and to the right the great arc of a rainbow reached across the sky. During the afternoon they were over Cape Breton, and as they left Newfoundland behind them the dusk rose. Ahead of them now was the Atlantic and growing darkness; the main part of the journey had begun. The engines were running smoothly, and Balchen's face as he sat at the controls was relaxed. Byrd turned to Noville.

'How's the fuel consumption? Have you checked it?'

Noville scribbled something on a notebook and handed the piece of paper to Byrd. Byrd read it and frowned. Then he looked up at Noville and asked: 'Are you sure your calculations are correct?'

'Why, yes.'

Byrd looked at him, opened his mouth as though to say something more, but then kept quiet instead. 'Forty gallons an hour!' he thought anxiously. At that rate their petrol would be exhausted before they reached Europe, which meant that they would come down in the sea, which meant . . . For the *America* was far too heavy to float for long. Byrd did some hard thinking. What had gone wrong? He had carefully calculated the consumption, and they should have had plenty of fuel to take them to Paris. There must be a leak in a feed-pipe somewhere.

Byrd did not want to alarm his companions. Their morale was almost more important than their physical fitness. To raise doubts in their minds already, when no more than about a quarter of the flight lay behind, might upset them. Byrd looked at their calm, confident faces, and decided to leave it that way for the time being. Later on there would still be plenty of time to turn back if it became unavoidable. In an hour he would get Noville to calculate the fuel consumption again, and then he would make his decision.

But he hadn't to wait for an hour, for after a while Noville leant over to him.

'I seem to have made a mistake after all,' he said sheepishly, and he handed Byrd another piece of paper with his scribbled calculations.

Byrd looked at it, and then did his best to conceal his satisfaction, just as he had concealed his anxiety previously. A surge of confidence rose in him now; there would certainly be enough fuel to take them to Paris at this rate of consumption.

In Paris they were expecting Byrd's arrival with equal confidence, and for a number of reasons. First of all the success of Lindbergh and then of Chamberlin and Levine in crossing the Atlantic had done a good deal to counteract the depression caused by the tragic loss of Nungesser and Coli. The successful crossings so close together seemed to prove that at least the transatlantic flight in the west–east direction was not too difficult with the sort of planes available in 1927; and they had particular confidence in a man like Byrd, an experienced airman and an outstanding navigator who, only the previous year, had flown to the North Pole with his friend Floyd Bennett. What predisposed the French in his favour was that he had chosen Paris as his objective rather than some other European capital, and also that he had promised to keep a weather eye open for the slightest sign of *L'Oiseau Blanc* on the way. No one had much hope, but the French were grateful for the thought.

Therefore towards evening on June 30th, crowds of Parisians on foot and in motor-cars began to make their way to Le Bourget once again to welcome another American flyer and one they already knew by reputation. This time they were not moved by that curiosity and half-concealed anxiety which had filled them when they had gone out there to welcome Lindbergh. This time they were in no doubt; they were quite confident that Byrd and his companions would make the journey safely; and by eight o'clock, when it was already dark, the cars on their way to Le Bourget moved forward almost bumper to bumper with their headlights on. From above it must have looked like a long, illuminated caterpillar meandering through the countryside.

At Le Bourget there was an atmosphere of carnival. Searchlights rose straight into the air like white columns, and now and again one of them swept round over the ground, lighting up the heads of the crowd, the waiting police and soldiers, the great hangars and the wings of planes standing on the tarmac. From time to time a rocket raced into the sky and burst, a welcoming signal for Byrd and his men.

Newspaper sellers were going around amongst the crowds with the latest editions of the evening papers. Byrd had been giving regular reports of his progress. The French transatlantic liner *Paris* had received one: 'Flying at 10,000 feet amidst thick fog. Very cold.' The regularity of those reports was encouraging, for Byrd and his fellow airmen had not had the best of weathers for their flight. However, there was nothing to worry about. In fact Byrd himself had said that bad weather conditions would not upset him. He was prepared for them. He and his men were not carrying out a daring hop for the sheer glory of it; they were soberly paving the way for the transatlantic passenger-carrying air services of the future, and those services would have to operate in fair weather and in foul—within reason at least. There would be no sense in a transatlantic airline which had to suspend its service very time the weather was poor. Regularity was the thing, just as it was on the railways. And, furthermore, when a man of Byrd's experience talked like that, he knew what he was doing.

The cargo-boat *Tuscaloosa City* picked up another message: 'All's well!' And then the *America* was sighted over Land's End. She had made the transatlantic crossing, and within a very short time now she ought to reach the French coast at Cherbourg and turn inland up the Seine estuary to the capital. Wireless operators were listening in eagerly, and thousands of observers along the route had their binoculars glued to the sky to spot the *America* as soon as she appeared over the horizon. It was quite true that visibility was rather poor, but it was to be hoped that once over France Byrd would come down low enough for watchers to glimpse his machine.

But two hours went by after the *America* was sighted over Land's End, and still none of the watchers in France had caught sight of her. Regretfully they put their binoculars away at last.

Visibility had become impossible, and, in any case, the *America* must have passed over so high that they had neither seen nor heard her.

The wireless operators were not so certain. They were tuning in anxiously to catch the slightest message from the *America* and then one of them began to scribble hastily on his note-block.

'From Byrd?' demanded a colleague excitedly. The fortunate operator nodded. At the end of the message he took off his head-phones.

'Where is he now?'

'He must be turning back to America.'

That sounded like a very bad joke, but the operator handed over his message, and it wasn't at all funny. Byrd had signalled his position—and it was at sea 160 miles south-west of Ushant.

'What on earth can he be doing there?' exclaimed one of the operators.

It was a fair question. Why had Byrd made that détour? He must have approached the French coast and then turned away again, which was extraordinary in view of the fact that Byrd had soberly declared that his aim was to approach as near as possible to the conditions of a commercial flight, and to take no unnecessary risks whatever or to try to set up any records of any kind.

The message was short, and there were no details. The W/T men excitedly discussed the possible reason for such behaviour on Byrd's part, but they could come to no plausible conclusion. The thing was just a mystery, and they would have to wait in patience until he himself provided the solution.

'Perhaps he's got sufficient fuel left to try one or two ways of approaching the coast, and wants to find out which is the most favourable, Cherbourg or Brest.' suggested someone hopefully.

The others would have liked to believe it, but they couldn't persuade themselves. In the meantime there was no further message. As far as Byrd was concerned the ether was empty.

Cherbourg and Paris were now both listening intently. At 20.30 hours they received a message; not from Byrd but from French naval headquarters at Brest to the effect that the *America* had just been sighted flying over the town at a height of about a thousand feet.

'Is the identity of the plane quite certain?' Paris demanded.

'Beyond all question,' came the reply. 'She gave her own identity.'

This message caused great relief; at least Byrd and his men were safe. It would be possible to find out later what he had been up to; for the moment the important thing was that he had arrived safely over French territory, and that he would soon be in the capital. At Le Bourget loudspeakers gave the news to the waiting crowds. Still more searchlights were switched on, and from 22.00 hours onward rockets were hissing into the sky regularly and causing ahs! and ohs! amongst the crowds. There was cloud cover everywhere now, and it was low, very low.

'Lindbergh had better luck with the weather,' someone said, and it was true. The waiting people remembered the clear sky and the bursting white rockets which had welcomed him to Paris. Rain was now beating down on the roofs of the hangars and the aerodrome buildings, and soaking the airfield. By 22.30 hours rockets were going up more frequently and far less regularly; it was almost as though panic were threatening. Searchlights were vainly trying to pierce the clouds first here and then there, almost desperately as though to open the way to a plane in trouble.

By 23.00 hours there was a rumour amongst the crowd that despite constant messages from land stations there was no news whatever of Byrd, and no signs of life from his machine.

'Still no sign of the Eiffel Tower light?'
'None at all.'
Rain was beating heavily against the cabin windows of the *America*. It couldn't be heard, on account of the greater noise

of the engines, but it was so heavy that there was practically no visibility at all. The water ran down the glass, and Byrd and his men felt as though they were imprisoned in a flying aquarium.

'That's dirty weather, if you like,' someone said.

Byrd didn't like it, but nevertheless that wasn't what was making him anxious. According to his calculations they ought to be over Paris already, and he circled round in the hope of spotting the lights of Le Bourget. But there was no break in the darkness, and when he switched on their own searchlight he could see nothing but rainclouds swirling in the gusts of wind. It was difficult to believe that there was any world outside this rain-sodden blanket of cloud. He checked the compass —the course seemed accurate enough.

'What's the time?' he asked.

'00.45 hours,' came the reply.

'Send out a signal that we believe ourselves to be circling over Paris, but are unable to see the ground.'

'We've drawn in the aerial, for fear it might get caught in trees,' Noville pointed out.

'We still ought to be able to send and receive on short waves.'

He was right there, and Le Bourget began to receive distinct short-wave messages from the *America* saying that she was circling but that no sign of the ground could be seen and no ground lights. The messages gradually became fainter and less distinct, but still clear enough to hear the international air S.O.S. . . . P.A.N. 'Why don't they say exactly what's wrong?' the men listening down below were wondering. 'Is there anything wrong with their engines? Are they running short of fuel?' Anxiously the watchers studied the heavy cloud cover which cut them off from Byrd and his companions and made it impossible to discover just what was wrong on board the *America*.

'The depressing thing is that we can't do a thing for them,' exclaimed one of the watchers. 'Even if we sent up planes to look for them, what good would that do—even if they found them? At sea, when a ship's in trouble another ship can help, but in the air . . .'

In the meantime the distress signals continued until at last they ceased altogether.

'Still no sign?' asked Byrd anxiously.

'Can't see a thing.'

It was 01.00 hours, and Byrd thought over the situation. He had enough fuel left to keep in the air until daylight, provided that the engines didn't let him down between now and then. If they could stay up safely until they could see they would be able to sight some landmark or other. For the moment there was just nothing to be done but circle round and hope for the best; a clear patch in the clouds, for example. And shortly after that it did look as though the darkness was lightening a little to starboard. The clouds were still rolling rapidly, but there was a break, and enough light to see.

'Good God, look!'

The four men who had believed themselves to be circling over Paris now saw the rolling sea beneath them, and for a moment or two each man wondered whether it was the sort of hallucination you suffered from sometimes when you were very, very tired and nearing exhaustion. But they all saw it, and there was no further doubt about it. Instead of the Eiffel Tower they had been hoping to see, there was the ocean, and a beach, and farther back houses and hotels with tables and big sunshades outside.

No one had any idea where it was, and what seaside resort they were looking down on. They were lost, and it was quite clear now that their compass must be out of order.

'I ought to have guessed it,' murmured Byrd.

On the way over he had noticed that the compass was behaving erratically, probably on account of the metallic mass of spare petrol cans, and he had had to correct his course more than once, particularly after leaving the English coast when he had found himself off Ushant instead of approaching Cherbourg as he had thought. It was that involuntary deviation which had so amazed the French W/T men.

The mist and clouds had closed in again, and the coast beneath them was out of sight. More by guess than any certainty Byrd altered course a few points to port and then did his best to think the situation out calmly. A landing at Le Bourget was out of the question now: there just wasn't enough fuel to take him back that far, even if he could find his way. They would have to land, and fairly soon. They might come down on the sands, for example, though as far as they had been able to see, the tide was in. 'All right,' said Byrd, 'if we can't land we'll have to go down in the sea.'

'There's a danger of capsizing if we do that,' said Noville.

'I know, but is there any alternative?' asked Byrd. 'It's gone half-past two, and the tanks are almost empty.'

They decided to go down and chance it; indeed, it was true that they had no alternative. They turned back to the seaside resort they had seen before, and by good luck the break in the clouds was still there—a bit of luck amidst all the bad luck! There was a small lighthouse at the end of a jetty, and the *America* circled above it for a while before Byrd gave the signal to Balchen, who was at the controls and who now turned the plane's nose down. They all braced themselves for the shock, and wondered whether they really were coming down in the water, for the cloud had rapidly closed in again, and they could no longer see. Byrd fired a red signal rocket, but the light it gave as it burst lit up nothing but cloud and impenetrable mist.

One of the engines began to knock as they went down, and the remaining petrol rushed forward to one end of the tank. Byrd was leaning out to starboard peering into the mist, but seeing nothing. Balchen, at the controls, read out the altimeter recordings: 'Fifty, forty, thirty, twenty . . .' Were they going down towards the sea or the land, perhaps into the roofs of houses? Balchen lifted the plane's nose a little. He was sweating like a bull, but he was calm. 'Ten. Zero!'

And at that moment the roar and stutter of the engines was joined by another sound—the rush of water against the fuselage! At the same time there was a violent shock and they were flung forward. Noville saw Byrd disappear, and then he knocked his own head against the main tank and lost consciousness for a moment. When he came to he could see no sign of any of the others. The *America* was in the water, floating with her tail in the air. Fortunately the sea was calm. Then he saw first Byrd and afterwards the other two, Balchen and Acosta, in the water, and he helped them climb onto the wings.

They were all grinning wryly now and congratulating themselves on being alive, and then they noticed that they couldn't hear each other, although everything except the soughing of the sea was silent now. The noise of the engines had deafened them.

Byrd made a sign that they must get ashore, and they dragged out the rubber dinghy and inflated it. Byrd took the mail-bag they had been carrying, and got into the dinghy with the others, then they paddled towards where they could see a light on shore. Within a quarter of an hour they landed and found themselves staggering up a sandy incline. Their troubles were not altogether over, and it took them an hour before they could find anyone in the sleeping village to attend to them. But once the villagers realized what had happened and who they were they were welcomed with open arms 'like sons coming home from the war'.

They had come down at Ver-sur-Mer, they discovered, and the remembrance of their welcome there after a flight which had been far more exciting and dangerous than his flight over the North Pole so impressed Byrd that subsequently when he was on his famous Antarctic expedition he named one of his bases 'Ver-sur-Mer'.

8

Atlantic Tragedy Again

'I HEAR Lindbergh has gone back to the States by boat. I shall go back by air.'

It was Charles A. Levine speaking. He had been in Paris for a month since his successful transatlantic crossing with Chamberlin, and there had been a good deal of talk about the two and their relationship, which had apparently not been altogether smooth. Levine was not an experienced flyer, and could only just about manage the controls; Chamberlin felt that as the experienced flyer, he was being interfered with, and apparently he was not keen on flying back with Levine, who was therefore looking round for another pilot. He asked the Frenchman Maurice Drouhin, who was preparing to attempt the east–west crossing with Joseph Le Brix. Drouhin agreed in principle, but he insisted on a proper contract, which Levine seemed in no hurry to sign.

There were others preparing to make the attempt too; for example Costes and Givan, who proposed to make the flight in their *Oiseau Bleu* and succeed where Nungesser and Coli had failed. Then there were Germans in the field, in particular Baron von Huenefeld, Hönnicke, Loose and Risticz; also three Englishmen, Courtney (who proposed to use a hydroplane), Hamilton and Minchin. On the other side of the Atlantic, Lloyd Berthaud was preparing to make another transatlantic flight from west to east.

The month of July passed. The flyers carried out their trials and eagerly studied the meteorological reports, but these were uniformly unfavourable—the Atlantic seemed to provide nothing but thoroughly discouraging troughs of depression.

Most of the flyers were tight-lipped about it all, but not so Levine, who kept the newspapers on their toes. One day he would decide to go with Drouhin as pilot; then he would decide that Drouhin wouldn't do, only to change his mind again. One day he would be exuding confidence; the next day he would be down in the dumps. One day he would be on good terms with Drouhin, the next day they would be squabbling. People began to wonder whether he would ever make the attempt at all—and in any case didn't think much of the chances of a flight arranged in such conditions.

In the meantime the weather reports remained discouraging, and the German flyers lost patience and started off on August 14th in two machines. But although they may have lost their patience they didn't lose their heads altogether. A few hours' flight convinced the first crew that the weather conditions were hopeless, so, having got as far as Ireland, they turned back. The second crew got no farther than Bremen. Very wise decisions they were, since for the time being the elements were decidedly hostile to all transatlantic flying.

On August 24th, however, the weather reports were more favourable, and taking advantage of the improvement William Brock and Edward Schlee started on a west–east transatlantic flight from Newfoundland, touching down safely at Croydon— the fourth non-stop air crossing—on the first stage of a round-the-world flight. They were welcomed warmly, of course, but the public attention was largely concentrated on something more sensational now. West to east flights would obviously soon become ten a penny; it was the east–west flight which captured the imagination—with the result that a fine performance did not get all the attention it deserved.

In France hopes were pinned chiefly on Costes, who was preparing to do the east–west flight with Le Brix in a machine called the *Nungesser and Coli* in honour of the two French flyers who had tried so gallantly and failed. In addition, Costes looked the most likely man for the job; he was experienced and capable, intelligent and resourceful—and perhaps precisely because he was all these things, he was not going in for much advance publicity. Levine, on the other hand, was still causing the press to occupy itself a good deal with him and his utterances. By this time poor Drouhin was beginning to regret that he had ever got tangled with the loquacious, irritable and dogmatic American, who seemed determined to provide a little unconscious comic relief in a drama which was still full of enigmas, danger and tragedy. He got into a brawl with a friend of Drouhin's on Le Bourget airfield, tried to get Drouhin to take his friends up on pleasure trips, which Drouhin refused to do—and finally the whole relationship ended in recriminations and litigation. On August 30th, without saying a word to a soul, the astonishing Levine managed to take off on his own in the *Miss Columbia* and get to Croydon, where he nearly crashed her. And after he had been in London a short while he announced that he had fixed up with a British pilot named Highcliffe to fly back with him over the Atlantic.

'I'm fed up with the French,' he announced. 'They've been getting at me from the start just because I didn't land in Paris first.'

The next candidate for transatlantic honours seemed to be Lloyd Berthaud, one of the Columbia Aircraft Corporation's old pilots, who was proposing to fly from New York to Rome. He was a fine pilot, he was well equipped and he had prepared his undertaking carefully, so his chances of success looked good. However, the British flyers Hamilton and Minchin actually got away first, flying a big monoplane, the *Saint Raphael*. They wanted to make the first east–west crossing, and in order to cut down the distance as far as possible they started from Upavon in Cornwall. They took a passenger with them: Princess Loewenstein Wertheim, who at the age of sixty-one proposed to be the first woman to fly the Atlantic— and from east to west too! She wore a blue leather flying outfit and suède boots, and her baggage consisted of two handbags, a basket of food and two hat-boxes.

The mechanics were engaged in putting the final touches to the engines, but even when they had finished and reported that everything was in order, the sign for the take-off was not given. The flyers seemed to be waiting for something, and after a while a motor-car drove through the rain on to the muddy airfield with the Archbishop of Cardiff and his acolytes. The archbishop blessed the plane and sprinkled holy water on to it, whilst the Princess stood with bowed head and joined hands and prayed silently. Ten minutes after the short ceremony the monoplane took off and disappeared into the mist, its course set for Newfoundland.

The plane was sighted out at sea by a tanker, but then no more was heard of it until its wreckage was found by another vessel. The Atlantic had claimed three more victims.

Neither that nor the previous tragedies discouraged the other aviators, and two days later, when it was already known that the monoplane was lost, the two French flyers Givion and Corbu took off from Le Bourget on the third attempt to fly the Atlantic from east to west. Three hours later they touched down at Le Bourget; they had found that their plane was so overloaded with its supplementary fuel that they could not gain sufficient height.

The next day the British flyer Courtney took off from Plymouth, flying a hydroplane, but was forced down at Corunna, fortunately without sustaining personal injuries. Then on September 7th came the long-awaited news that Lloyd Berthaud had taken off at 13.25 hours on his flight to Rome. It was an ambitious undertaking: 3,850 miles non-stop. The plane, *Old Glory*, was powered by a single engine developing 450 h.p., and there were three men on board, the others being the co-pilot Hill and a journalist named Payne (incidentally, the flight was being financed by the newspaper magnate Hearst). The plane was equipped with wireless, as well as an automatic device for sending out distress signals in the event of a forced landing, while in addition to carefully-chosen provisions, there was an apparatus for distilling sea water, and an inflatable rubber dinghy. There was also something a little odd: a wreath with a ribbon inscribed 'To Nungesser and Coli—You showed us the way; we are following'. Of course, Nungesser and Coli had flown in the other direction. However . . .

'We are going to drop it in mid-Atlantic in honour of the two French flyers,' explained Berthaud.

He had chosen a route rather farther to the south than the one flown by Lindbergh, to give him and his crew the advantage of flying along frequented sea lanes so that if anything did go wrong they could hope for assistance. On September 7th a number of vessels crossing the Atlantic did spot *Old Glory*, and all seemed well. It looked as though Berthaud had drawn a winning ticket in the transatlantic flying lottery.

During the night W/T officers on board all the ships in the neighbourhood listened carefully for any news of *Old Glory*, and round about midnight there were a number whose course through the rather heavy seas which were being churned up by a strong westerly wind gave them a chance of spotting the aeroplane. On the bridges the look-outs kept an eye open for the navigation lights of Berthaud's plane, but there was a low cloud ceiling, and they had little hope of seeing anything.

The wireless officer on board the *Transsylvania* was one of those keeping vigil, but all he could hear was the sound of heavy waves dashing against the vessel, the swish of spray hitting against the glass of his cabin scuttle, and the howling of the wind through the rigging and the aerials. It was very dirty weather, and the thought of the flyers out there in it made him appreciate the warmth and comfort of his own cabin, where he could sit at his ease and listen to signs of life from all over the world: time signals, messages, conversations between various stations, and so on. But the one thing he hadn't managed to hear so far was anything from Berthaud and his *Old Glory*.

Then he began to pick up a message: '*Old Glory* calling, *Old Glory* calling.' Then came the position, followed, to the

operator's dismay, by P.A.N., the S.O.S. signal of the air. He
hurriedly scribbled the message on his pad and hurried with it
to the bridge. The high wind slammed the door of his cabin
to behind him. The weather seemed to be getting worse
instead of better. It was to be hoped that *Old Glory* would be
able to keep in the air, for to come down in this would mean
disaster.

The *Transsylvania* ploughed through the storm towards the
position indicated. She was not the only ship to be hurrying
in that direction. There was the *California*, for example, and
five other transatlantic liners; they all altered course to go to
the rescue. On the bridges of all of them were men who
anxiously searched the horizon in the direction indicated. The
sea was very heavy now; green, rolling and flecked with foam.
If the flyers had been forced to come down in that . . . It took
the *Transsylvania* six hours to reach the position indicated in
the last message picked up from *Old Glory*. She was better
placed than the other vessels, and she was in the neighbourhood
by dawn.

The captain of the *Transsylvania* quartered the whole area
systematically, zig-zagging here and there and circling round
a great area. Gradually other vessels steamed up to help in the
search, and from the bridge of the *Transsylvania* their masts
and superstructures could be sighted from time to time
according to the course of the search. At the end of six hours
there was no sign of *Old Glory*. The search was kept up for
another six hours, and still there was no result.

The position Berthaud had given made the search easier,
and defined its area fairly clearly; but once that particular area
had been throughly searched there was no hope left that the
plane might have remained afloat after all. So after twelve
hours' intensive search, the various ships reluctantly steamed
back on to their own courses and continued their journeys.

During the following weeks fragments of wreckage were
sighted and fished out of the sea, and there was little doubt
that these were all that would ever be found of Lloyd Berthaud

and his two companions. The pathetic wreath which had been meant for Nungesser and Coli now served for three more men who had died in the same way.

Once again the news of the disaster did nothing to prevent the next flyers from taking their chance. Two days later two British flyers named Tully and Metcalfe took off in their plane, the *Sir John Carling*. They were on their way to London—no one had as yet flown there non-stop from New York. They left Roosevelt Field and were last sighted over Newfoundland. After that they disappeared out to sea over the Atlantic, and at Croydon aerodrome a watch was kept for them—in vain. They were never heard of again.

This new disaster sobered public opinion, and voices began to be raised against what now seemed very like near-suicide. The U.S. Government actually forbade all transatlantic official flights. Newspaper men interviewed Lindbergh to canvass his opinion. 'Such flights should not be prohibited,' he replied. 'Men should still make them, but only after the most careful preparation.'

It was objected that a man like Byrd had certainly made careful preparations and taken every precaution, and nevertheless he and his companions had been lucky to escape with their lives. Without belittling his achievement, people began to feel that Lindbergh himself must have had a big slice of luck. The sensational press had even dubbed him 'the Flying Fool,' though in reality he was nothing of the sort; he had prepared his own flight most carefully, and he had certainly not flown 'by instinct', as had been said. On the contrary he had flown with the most up-to-date scientific navigational aids possible at the time for a small machine.

There was someone else whose views on this same subject the newspaper men were anxious to hear. Her name was Ruth Elder, and she had announced calmly that she intended to fly the Atlantic. Not as a passenger, but as the pilot. 'But, of course,' she added, 'first of all I must get my pilot's licence.' Apparently the fact that experienced pilots were losing their

lives over the Atlantic did not perturb her. In the end, however, she did not fly on her own but with an experienced
flyer named Haldeman.

In the meantime the weather remained unfavourable. The
British flyers MacIntosh and Fitzgerald did take advantage of
what seemed a change in the weather to take off from Dublin
to fly the Atlantic in the east–west direction, but it turned out
to have been a false hope of improvement, and after an hour
or two in the air they wisely turned back. As though to underline the wisdom of their decision it was reported that the
wreckage of a large plane had been found floating in the
Atlantic off the Irish coast.

On September 30th, Costes and Le Brix announced that as
there seemed little likelihood of any real improvement in the
weather now they would postpone their east–west flight until
the following year. The mercurial Levine gave up, too.
Instead of setting off to fly back to the States he took off with
his pilot Hinchliffe for India. They touched down in Rome,
where the old scenario began to unroll once more. Levine
quarrelled with Hinchliffe. For a while the continuation of the
flight seemed in doubt. Then they made it up again and took
off, but *Miss Columbia* lost height after the take-off and
crashed. Fortunately neither of the flyers was injured, but that
was the end of Levine's flying adventures.

The curtain seemed to have fallen on transatlantic flights for
the current year, and the general public felt relieved. Thirteen
men and a woman had lost their lives in various attempts, and
that was enough for the time being. Other subjects now began
to occupy the attention of newspaper readers. Then, on
October 12th, the attractive Miss Elder, twenty years old, took
off with her pilot in the *American Girl*, after having posed
smiling for a last photograph to gratify the numerous reporters
and press photographers who had been despatched post-haste
to the airfield to see her off. 'Fools rush in . . .' more than one
of them muttered. And the weather hadn't improved very
much either! But Haldeman was at least wise in his route: he

preferred to go via the Azores, which made the first stage of the journey shorter and the hope of being picked up in the event of failure more likely.

About six hundred miles out to sea a cargo boat sighted the plane. After that there were more sightings—after all, they were flying along a very frequented route. About 120 miles further on they were seen once more, and yet again another three hundred miles nearer their destination. It began to look as though an attempt made in circumstances which had discouraged more experienced flyers was going to succeed, and at Le Bourget they began preparation for receiving the *American Girl*—in both senses. The Parisians, always generous and impulsive, were touched at the thought of that young woman flying over the Atlantic, particularly as she had said that her one ambition was to see Paris! Eagerly the public was now waiting for further messages, and another one came.

On October 13th the tanker *Barendrecht* with course to Houston sighted a plane flying eastward. It was seven-fifteen in the morning when the officer of the watch first spotted her.

'It can only be the *American Girl*,' he exclaimed, and he gave instructions to chalk the position on deck so that the flyers could know exactly where they were. Sure enough the plane, which had seen them too, came down to take a closer look—and to drop a message on board. The plane flew low over the masts against the wind and a small weighted bag containing the message dropped neatly on to the deck. Hurriedly it was opened and the message read: 'How far are we from the nearest land?' At the instructions of the officer of the watch a seaman hurriedly wrote in great letters on the deck: '360 miles to the Azores', with an arrow indicating the direction.

The plane turned about, came back, flew low and obviously read the message. Then it gained height and flew on.

The captain of the *Barendrecht*, who was on the bridge, said, 'It was a bit odd they didn't ask their position, but just wanted to know how far they were from the nearest land.'

Then they noticed that the plane—which the sailors of the

Barendrecht had cheered vociferously—didn't seem to be able to decide in which direction to fly; to the Azores or direct to Europe.

'I shouldn't have thought they had all that much petrol to spare,' said the captain. 'A pity we can't let them have some of ours; we'd never miss it.'

Then, unexpectedly, the plane turned back and came down very close to the surface of the sea on a parallel course to that of the tanker.

'What are they up to now?' exclaimed the captain.

'They're coming down, that's what they are, sir,' said the officer of the watch.

'Lower a boat,' ordered the captain, and men ran to man the near-side boat, whilst he pulled the engine-room telegraph over to 'Stop'. The tanker was moving forward only under her own momentum, and the plane touched down amidst a tremendous flurry of spray. The sound of its engine increased for a moment, and then ceased altogether; there the machine floated. Two figures climbed out of the cabin on to the nearest wing and began waving their arms. The smaller figure was obviously Miss Elder. The lifeboat was already in the water and its crew were pulling strongly towards the plane—it wasn't a hydroplane and it couldn't stay on the surface for long. Ten minutes later the two flyers were safely on board the *Barendrecht*.

'What happened to you?' the captain inquired.

'Pressure had fallen to zero. We should never have been able to make Europe. A feed-pipe burst, I expect.'

They had been very lucky to be saved. True, the route was followed by a good many ships, but the Atlantic is a large expanse of water. And just how lucky they had been the captain himself told them.

'By rights we ought to have been six hundred miles away from here, but we had boiler trouble and were held up forty-eight hours at Rotterdam. But for that, the sea in these parts would have been empty—except for you.'

At least Ruth Elder and her pilot Haldeman had broken the long-distance record for a flight over the sea: 2,733 miles! And the year 1927, a year of triumph and disaster over the Atlantic, ended with the photograph of a smiling American girl in all the newspapers, and did something to make people forget the previous photographs of Nungesser and Coli and all the others who had lost their lives. It was also proof that flyers had not given up.

9

Touch and Go for the 'Bremen'

'WHAT does the Canadian weather bureau say?'
        'Storm approaching from the east over Nova Scotia.'
'And Washington?'
'High wind and rain from the north of Cape Hatteras to Boston.'

The three men eagerly studied all the weather reports concerning the areas that interested them. None of them was promising.

'We should have to fight against headwinds for perhaps half the way, that means.'

The speaker was Baron Günther von Huenefeld. The two men were Hauptmann (Captain) Köhl, formerly of the German Air Force, and Major James Fitzmaurice of the Irish Free State Army. The three proposed to fly from Baldonnel, Dublin's aerodrome, to New York, at the same time making the first east-to-west Atlantic crossing. On August 14th, 1927, Baron von Huenefeld had been in the air twenty-two hours with Köhl and Loose in his plane, the *Bremen*, and had then been forced to return on account of bad weather and impenetrable mist. It was April 11th, 1928, now; he and Köhl had flown from Germany to Dublin—and they had already been waiting for a fortnight in the hope that the weather over the Atlantic would change for the better and give them the chance they were after. That was longer than they had expected, and they were beginning to grow impatient.

A month previously another pilot had been in much the same position, and he had lost patience. No less than twelve transatlantic flights were in course of preparation, and he was anxious to get off ahead of the others. He was Hinchliffe, the man who had piloted Levine and crashed with the *Miss Columbia* in Rome; he had another plane now, the *Adventure*. Although he was known to be preparing a long-distance flight, everyone thought he was going to try for India again. Actually his intention was to attempt the transatlantic crossing from east to west.

On March 13th he took off from Cranwell airfield with an airwoman, Miss MacKay, as his companion. The plane was sighted over Cork flying westward through a storm, and observers thought that Hinchliffe would put back, because the weather was so bad. But Hinchliffe did not put back; nothing more was ever heard of him or his plane, or Miss MacKay, who was the second woman victim of transatlantic flying. Thus the 1928 transatlantic flying season opened with a disaster.

In the meantime the French flyers Dettroyat, Paillard and Drouhin (the latter with a three-engined plane, specially designed by the well-known aero-engineer Couzinet, called the *Arc-en-Ciel*), and the Germans Baron von Huenefeld and Köhl, with the Irish officer Fitzmaurice, all intended to make the east–west attempt. The Baron and his crew were the farthest advanced; they were actually, so to speak, on their way—they had got as far as Ireland. But the weather forecasts were uniformly discouraging, and they hesitated.

And then unexpectedly an improvement was forecast—not over the whole route, and the U.S. bulletins remained pessimistic, but for perhaps a third of the way. The three men went into conference. Should they risk it? From Ireland to Newfoundland was the shortest direct distance over the Atlantic, and the *Bremen* had already demonstrated that she could—if all went well—stay in the air for forty-five hours at a stretch, which meant that they had a good chance of succeeding despite the weather.

'Headwinds for at least half the flight,' repeated von Huenefeld.

Fitzmaurice said nothing. The evening before he had told a friend that he would leave the decision to the Germans, though he thought you really needed a three-engined plane with enough fuel for at least sixty hours to go sure. In this weather he felt more than ever that he was right. But if the Germans went he'd certainly go.

'If we wait much longer for favourable weather I don't think we'll ever get away at all,' said Köhl finally.

They studied the weather bulletins again. Behind the dry, scientific and laconic notes they could sense mist, squalls, contrary winds and icing.

'At least we can try,' said the Baron. 'We've already been hanging around here for a couple of weeks. That's a bit too much.'

He looked at his two companions.

'I vote we start tomorrow,' he said.

The other two nodded, and they all shook hands on it.

The following morning, when the last stars were still in the sky, over five hundred people were assembled at Baldonnel airfield to see the take-off. There was a chilly north wind, but at least the weather was clear. Unfortunately the fine patch was purely local, but at least it raised everyone's spirits and seemed a good omen for the flight. The German Consul was there to see his compatriots off, and representatives of the Irish Free State Government. Of the three flyers, only Baron von Huenefeld was on the airfield, talking to the mechanics servicing the *Bremen*. Fitzmaurice and Köhl did not arrive until a little later; they had both been to early Mass at a nearby church, and had taken communion.

When they arrived Fitzmaurice put an ivory crucifix into the cabin, which had been specially blessed for the flight. The three flyers then shook hands with a good many of those who had come to see them off, and then they climbed into the plane, an all-metal Junkers. The propeller was already turning, and the engine was warming up. Then storm clouds began to roll over and the sky darkened. But there was no question of any further postponement, and with Köhl at the controls the *Bremen* began to move down the runway, quickly gathering speed. At about a thousand yards distance it left the ground; then it descended again, ran a little farther, and finally took off easily. The cheers of the waiting crowd were drowned in the roar of a bombing plane which took off to escort the *Bremen* out to sea. After about a quarter of an hour the military plane returned.

'Engine trouble?' officials asked.

'No, but we lost sight of the *Bremen* very quickly. Visibility is very poor. They'll have a job right from the start. I'm not at all sure whether they'll be able to go on.'

But they went on. Köhl had taken his plane up above the mist and cloud cover, and the sea below them was invisible except where now and again there was a break in the clouds.

'I think the weather's improving,' said von Huenefeld optimistically.

The wind had changed to the south-east, and seemed to be dispersing the mist. In fact after a while the mist was blown away, and the broad expanse of the Atlantic appeared below them, with a heavy swell running and white horses rearing and tossing along the crests of the waves. The three flyers looked down in silence at the enemy they had challenged, and they thought of all the other men—and women—who had done the same and paid for it with their lives—Highcliffe and his companion so very recently. . . . Fitzmaurice checked the fuel consumption. The speed was just a hundred miles an hour, and everything was normal. Köhl at the controls had succeeded in taking the *Bremen* up higher now.

Baron von Huenefeld looked out at the wings of his plane, which had been covered with paraffin to hinder the formation of ice. It actually was his plane; he had paid for it and he was defraying all the costs of the flight out of his own pocket, for the German Government had regarded the attempt as too risky to justify the expenditure of government money on it. Perhaps the fact that Baron von Huenefeld was a monarchist who made no secret of his political opinions had contributed to bringing about the refusal of the republican authorities.

The daring baron had not let that discourage him. He had worked hard and with determination to carry out what he regarded as the great task of his life—this transatlantic flight from east to west, and he was resolved to do everything possible to achieve what no man had as yet achieved. 'His greatest drama,' he called it, for he was also a playwright, and two of his pieces had already been performed in Germany. Many people regarded his attempt as folly, and feared that it would end in tragedy, but von Huenefeld had made his preparations carefully and taken every possible precaution, so that he was calmly confident of the outcome. Up to now luck had seemed on his side, as it so often is on the side of the brave man who is ready to act daringly, for the weather was not so bad as the forecasts had threatened, and the engine was behaving perfectly. The thrill of being on the way, of actually fighting the battle, caused a surge of elation to rise in him, and taking a note-block he began to scribble the first verse of a poem which had come into his head.

The *Bremen* had been in the air some hours, and over eleven hundred miles of the way was now behind them. A good deal of their fuel had already been consumed, and the plane was that much lighter. They were flying at about five thousand feet between two banks of violet cloud which gradually grew deeper and deeper in shade as night fell.

'Fitz, be a good fellow, switch on, will you?' said Köhl. 'I can't see very well.'

Fitzmaurice switched on, but the instrument panel still remained unlighted. He switched off and checked the connections and the fuses. Everything seemed in order and he switched on again, but still without result. The matter wasn't serious, but it was a nuisance, and either von Huenefeld or Fitzmaurice had to shine a torch on the compass face for Köhl to see and keep the plane on its course.

When they were still about six hundred miles from their destination, with more than two-thirds of their journey already behind them, the weather grew thick and the west wind rose and hindered their progress. The reduction of speed was very obvious.

'What are we doing now, Fitz?' asked von Huenefeld, a little anxiously.

'Not much more than sixty,' replied the lanky Irishman.

At that rate there was obviously a danger that the *Bremen* would not have enough fuel to reach New York. Von Huenefeld noted their position and bent over the map. It was questionable whether they would even be able to reach the coast. The temperature in the cabin was sinking noticeably, and he feared the formation of ice on the wings. The wings were covered with paraffin, it was true, but if it grew cold enough that might not be sufficient to prevent ice formation—in which case the weight of the plane would be increased and their speed still further reduced. Von Huenefeld pushed back the window of the cockpit and examined the wings in the light of his torch. There were one or two sinister-looking shining patches.

'We'd better go down a bit, Hermann,' he said to Köhl.

At that moment the *Bremen* did go down, but not in answer to the controls; and looking at Köhl, von Huenefeld could see that he was doing his best to control the sudden drop of perhaps three hundred feet or so. The machine shuddered, lurched and then recovered its level flight.

'Air pocket,' said Köhl laconically.

But it was more the kind of vortex caused by a depression, and was likely to be followed by others. A little later the same thing happened again: the *Bremen* suddenly and violently lost height, and Köhl had his work cut out to regain control of the machine and flatten out.

'What's the altitude now?' demanded von Huenefeld.

'Just over sixteen hundred feet, skipper,' said Fitzmaurice.

'I think that's too low. We'll have to get her up a bit, Hermann.'

'Easier said than done,' grunted Köhl.

Sudden squalls of wind tended to press the machine down still lower as though to force them into the sea. The engine started to roar; then it began to cough, but finally it resumed its normal running.

'The coast of Newfoundland must be quite near now,' said von Huenefeld after a swift calculation, 'and a very good thing too.' By dawn, which was not far off, they ought to be over Newfoundland, and if necessary they would at least be able to make a forced landing. 'Three hundred miles to go,' he added.

'If the weather stays like this we shan't even see it,' said Fitzmaurice, pointing ahead to a whitish-grey mass.

'Is it mist?' asked von Huenefeld, peering out.

'It's worse than that,' returned the Irishman, 'it's snow.'

He was right. Snow would increase the weight of the plane even more than ice, and it would be impossible to evade it by rising to a greater altitude, for with the constant violent squalls which forced the *Bremen* down it was as much as Köhl could do to keep her clear of the water. The three men stared at the altimeter dial; its needle oscillated constantly, sometimes touching zero. Now and again they thought they could hear the sound of waves thrashing against the fuselage, and at any moment they feared the violent bump which would tell them they had hit the surface of the sea. After that the plane might stay afloat for a while, but not for long, and then . . . They hadn't even an inflatable dinghy with them.

During the hours of tense anxiety that followed, when the cold paralysed their muscles and a sense of helplessness oppressed them, they feared more than once that they could not emerge triumphant from this blind struggle against the wind, the snow and the sea. At last it grew lighter, and they were able to see out a little. In the rare breaks in the mist and cloud they eagerly sought for a sight of land, the 'new-found land' they were so anxious to find again; but they could see nothing.

'This cold and snow are abnormal even for these parts at
this time of the year,' said von Huenefeld. 'Are you quite sure
we're on the right course, Hermann?'

'Well, if the compass is in order we are. If it isn't, of
course . . .'

But was it? Something of the sort had happened to Byrd.
If his compass had been in order, he and his men would have
arrived safely in Paris instead of coming down in the sea and
nearly losing their lives; and perhaps something of the sort
had happened to those others who had not been lucky enough
to escape with their lives. If the weather had been clear it
might have been possible to identify landmarks, or to get into
touch with ships; but in this white obscurity it was hopeless.
If their compass were really out of order, then no matter how
long their engine still lasted they would crash into the sea in
the end.

The morning papers on April 13th made no mention of the
disquieting situation with regard to the *Bremen*: not once had
there been a sighting by any ship at sea, and from the other
side the meteorologists reported strong west winds with
squalls and snow. But the German midday papers published a
report that the *Bremen* had been sighted over Nova Scotia, and
the report was confirmed later on when the evening papers
appeared. In fact the newspapers reported that the two German
flyers, Baron von Huenefeld and Hauptmann Hermann Köhl,
with their Irish companion Major Fitzmaurice, had touched
down in New York accompanied by a squadron of U.S. army
planes. Crowds flocked on to the streets in Germany, and flags
were put out at the windows: a German plane had been the
first to make the east–west Atlantic crossing.

But when confirmation was sought in New York for this
report, there was bitter disappointment. It was not true that
the *Bremen* had landed there; the plane had not been seen since
that first sighting over Nova Scotia. The crowds in Berlin and
other German towns were suddenly sobered up, and it was

now feared that von Huenefeld's machine had suffered the same fate as *L'Oiseau Blanc*—which also had been falsely reported as arriving triumphantly in New York.

The night passed without further news. The U.S. authorities started a search off the coasts the next day, but without result. But then a report came from Labrador that a plane had crashed on the little island off Greenly, and it seemed likely that this was the missing *Bremen*.

'We must be over land now,' insisted von Huenefeld. The three men were tired and hungry, and chilled to the bone. It was only the instinct of self-preservation which made them hope on. Köhl stuck to the controls grimly and mastered his fatigue. They were flying at a height of about sixteen hundred feet amidst rain and snow clouds. The swiftly changing shapes of the clouds seemed menacing at times; it was almost as though giant hands were reaching out to crush the *Bremen*, and they were constantly being violently shaken by swift squalls of wind, rain and snow. Above them, around them, and below them was the same tumultuous mass of cloud, and neither sea nor land might have existed for all they could tell about either. They seemed to be fighting for their lives in endless white mist and cloud.

Baron von Huenefeld felt the hard mass of his pistol in his hip pocket. Sooner than die like a rat in this wretched trap, he would make an end of himself. He had deliberately risked his life on this flight; he would just as deliberately pay the forfeit. He looked at the other two. Fitzmaurice was still staring keenly out of the window, and Köhl was still at the controls. They were both Catholics; Köhl would stay at those controls until the tanks were completely empty and the *Bremen* plunged down to disaster. Suddenly Fitzmaurice interrupted the gloomy train of the baron's thoughts by suddenly turning away from the look-out window to him.

'Believe it or not, Von, but I caught a glimpse of the sea and a ship down there,' he said excitedly.

Looking down hurriedly they all saw it: something like the funnel of a ship—impossible to tell just what it was, the visibility was so poor. The odd thing was that it had been quite motionless. A ship fast in inshore ice, they thought; for in that rolling, tossing sea any ship would have been pitching and heaving. Köhl swung the plane round and returned to the spot, but this time they could see nothing. Köhl circled several times, but still to no purpose.

'I didn't imagine it,' said Fitzmaurice positively. 'It was a ship.'

The others were sure they had seen it too—or had thought they had seen it. . . . Perhaps Fitzmaurice had imagined it after all, and they had been so willing to see it that the suggestion had been enough. But they could certainly see nothing now, no matter how hard they stared out. And then after about five minutes there was a shadow down below.

'Dammit!' exclaimed Fitzmaurice. 'Don't tell me I'm mad. They're trees. It's a forest.'

For a moment they all hoped again, but the matter-of-fact Köhl poured cold water on the idea. 'A ship and a forest both in the same place? It doesn't make sense.'

But there were shadows of some sort, and between them were wide expanses of white, while farther away were what looked like hills.

'It can't be Nova Scotia,' said von Huenefeld.

For long periods the whirling snow robbed them of all visibility, but gradually the clouds and mist dissipated. Then they saw land beneath them; an island with pine trees, surrounded by a flat expanse of ice very different from the turbulent seas over which they had flown for so many hours. They stared unbelievingly at it, whilst their spirits rose at the thought that the sea had been left behind.

'Look!' exclaimed Fitzmaurice, 'that lighthouse there must have been the ship's funnel we thought we saw.'

Köhl was looking out for a good place to land now. He took the *Bremen* round the island and then over the ice.

'I think we'd better go down on the ice,' he said.

'Do you think it will bear our weight?' queried Fitzmaurice.

'If it doesn't we'll probably have time to jump,' returned Köhl, 'but it's our only chance. We've not got enough fuel to take us much farther; even if we had, we might fare worse.'

He took the *Bremen* down low and skimmed over the ice looking for a favourable spot to land. Then he put her down on a level stretch. The three men felt the front wheels touch the ice; then the tail wheel touched down and slithered from left to right. They went on over the ice in this zig-zag fashion for a few hundred yards, gradually slowing down until finally the *Bremen* was pulled up suddenly by an ice ridge and there was a long drawn-out cracking sound.

'The ice is giving way,' shouted von Huenefeld. 'Get ready to jump!'

But although it cracked, the ice held under the weight of the *Bremen*. Most of the cracking had been caused by the crushing of the undercarriage and the splitting of the propeller.

The three men remained for a while motionless in their cabin. Their fatigue and their pent-up fears seemed to have petrified them, and they hardly had strength enough or will-power enough to move their chilled limbs. Köhl had shut off the engine, and after thirty uninterrupted hours of its roar the silence seemed deafening; an inhuman and unreal silence which for a moment they hardly dared break by speaking. And, in any case, what was there to be said? For the moment they were so taken up by the fact that they were alive and no longer in the air that the thought of their success had not yet occurred to them. They were now the first men to have accomplished the difficult and dangerous east–west crossing of the Atlantic, but before they got that far in their minds they realized that perhaps they had only exchanged death by drowning for a slower death by exhaustion, cold and starvation in these icy and deserted wastes. For who would dream of looking for them in a place like this?

'What about that lighthouse?' said Köhl, who knew

perfectly well what the others were thinking—he had been thinking it himself. He realized that his hands were still gripping the controls, so he let go and relaxed.

For a moment they had forgotten that lighthouse they had taken for a ship's funnel. But it might have been abandoned, or its light might be under remote control.

'It's a sign of human life, anyway,' said von Huenefeld. 'I'll go and see.'

He climbed out of the cockpit and started to make his way across the ice in his thin-soled boots. Once or twice he stumbled and even fell, but he picked himself up again and pressed on towards the lighthouse; it was their only hope. If it proved to be deserted, his fate and that of his two companions would not be enviable. When he came within a hundred yards or so of it his sight became blurred and he could see nothing. Then his eyes focused again and he pressed on. He hardly dared hope, but he thought he could distinguish someone at the door. His feet were wet and numbed, and it was very rough going in his weak and exhausted condition. He closed his eyes for a moment or two and stood there, unable to go on. When he opened them again it was to see a woman making her way towards him.

'I saw you come down,' she said. 'Are you a Canadian?'

'No, a German. We've flown from Europe.'

'Good heavens!'

She supported him now as they made their way towards the lighthouse.

'Come into the kitchen and get those boots off; they're no good for these parts. I'll get you some sabots. Are you hungry?'

'I would have said yes a little while ago,' he replied, 'but to tell you the truth I don't know now.'

He looked at the woman. She was a Madame Le Templier, the wife of the French-Canadian keeper of the lighthouse. She busied herself heating up milk, and she fetched biscuits. It was difficult to believe that they were really and truly saved.

'Where exactly are we?' he asked.

Madame Le Templier looked astonished.

'Why, in Labrador, of course,' she said. 'On Greenly Island.'

'Labrador!' he thought—'well over a thousand miles away from New York!' That was odd. Köhl was an experienced pilot. He hadn't made any mistakes; he had kept the *Bremen* steadily on her course; and he wouldn't have made any navigation errors. That compass must have been out of order after all.

'People will be wondering what's happened to us,' he said aloud. 'Can one send a message of any sort from here?'

'My husband will send a message through for you when he gets back. Ah! I think that's him now.'

But it wasn't; it was Köhl and Fitzmaurice, almost staggering across the ice and at the end of their physical tether. They gratefully dropped into chairs in the good woman's kitchen and drank hot milk and ate biscuits almost in silence, still half-dazed by their ordeal and their narrow escape.

As soon as the news came through, a rescue expedition was organized to bring the flyers back to civilization. Two days later a small plane landed near the lighthouse and took off Fitzmaurice, leaving the news that two of America's greatest flyers, Floyd Bennett and Balchen, both close companions of the great Commander Byrd on his expeditions, were on the way. Floyd Bennett had flown with Byrd over the North Pole in 1926, and Balchen had piloted Byrd's transatlantic flight to Paris which had ended in the crash at Ver-sur-Mer.

Baron von Huenefeld wanted to stay and repair the *Bremen*, but he had to give up the idea, and it was almost a fortnight later that Balchen flew her to New York. Unfortunately at some time during the rescue flight Floyd Bennett caught a chill which turned into pneumonia, and he died—the only victim of the first successful east–west flight over the Atlantic.

10

Jean Mermoz and the Southern Route

O N October 10th, 1927, a large biplane stood on the runway
at Le Bourget. Written on its fuselage were two names
that no Frenchman could read without emotion: 'Nungesser
and Coli'—the first men to try the east–west flight across
the Atlantic.

The machine was that in which the well-known French
flyers Dieudonné Costes and Joseph Le Brix now proposed to
fly not the North, but the South Atlantic. Costes, the leader of
the flight, was of the opinion that in the present state of
aeronautical technique any flight across the North Atlantic
must be a gamble, particularly from east to west; as the best
of the weather had now gone; and it was the flight from Paris
to New York which primarily interested him. All the same, he
proposed to attempt something that no one else had as yet
succeeded in doing non-stop—a crossing of the South Atlantic.
Just in case of accidents, his Bréguet-Hispano with its 600 h.p.
engine would carry wireless and two inflatable rubber dinghies.

Costes and Le Brix flew non-stop from Le Bourget to Saint
Louis in Senegal, a distance of 2,850 miles, on the first stage of
their journey, and on October 14th they took off from there in
very good weather. Flying at a height of about ten thousand
feet they set course for Brazil, doing about 125 miles an hour.
Le Brix sent out messages at regular intervals, indicating that
all was going well, and in almost exactly eight hours after their
departure from St. Louis they touched down safely in Natal
in Brazil.

It was the start of a splendidly successful world tour, including Africa, Latin-America, the United States, the crossing of

the Pacific by ship, Japan, China, India and back to Paris, where they arrived on April 14th, 1928, having flown a total distance of 35,400 miles. It was a magnificent performance, and, of course, the greatest feat was the non-stop flight across the Atlantic from St. Louis to Natal, a distance of well over 2,000 miles. But no sooner was the record set up than other flyers were preparing to break it.

'You propose to fly non-stop from Italy to Brazil, I understand?'

'That is so. My machine, a Savoia with a 550 h.p. engine, is capable of doing between four and five thousand miles non-stop, and that should allow me sufficient margin. In addition I shall hope, of course, to break the long-distance flying record.'

A journalist was interviewing the Italian flyer Arturo Ferrarin the day before he and Major Del Prete proposed to take off from Montecelio airfield.

At dawn the following day, July 3rd, 1928, the Savoia made a good start. It was excellent weather—almost too good, for over Algeria the engine showed signs of overheating. Del Prete checked the temperatures: 198° F. for the water, 155° F. for the oil. Such temperatures were disturbing.

'It will be cooler when we get out to sea,' said Ferrarin optimistically.

In fact the sea breeze did bring a certain cooling with it, but it also brought a great deal of cloud, and Ferrarin was unable to rise above it. At eleven thousand feet clouds were still all around the plane, and, in addition, there were disturbing air vortices. But then at last they could see the Atlantic through the mist.

The sun was shining again now, and they put mile after mile behind them until at 16.00 hours on July 4th the low coastline of Brazil came into sight on the horizon. The two flyers turned southward, but running into storms they were forced to turn back and make for Natal, which, however, they failed to reach. Fuel shortage caused them to make a forced landing on the sands. By that time, however, they had been in the air forty-eight hours and had travelled a total distance of 4,413 miles, thus breaking the long-distance flying record set up by Chamberlin and Levine.

One year later, on March 24th, 1929, two Spanish flyers named Jimenez and Inglesias set off to beat this new record. They took off from Seville with the *Jesus del Gran Poder* to fly to Rio de Janeiro, a distance of 5,000 miles. They passed over the Cape Verde Islands on March 26th, and at dawn the next day they sighted the coast of Brazil. Unfortunately the weather was very bad; the sky was covered with tropical clouds which soon deprived the flyers of all visibility and forced them to land, which they did at 10.40 hours in Bahia.

'It was impossible to go on any further,' explained Jimenez, who seemed very exhausted. 'From Natal we had to fight the whole time against storms and headwinds which sometimes lowered our speed to fifty miles per hour.'

On December 5th, 1929, another plane took off from Cordova, piloted by the French flyer Challe and the Uruguayan Larre Borges, one of the Rio de Oro survivors. They crossed the greater part of the Atlantic without difficulty, but about 500 miles from the coast they ran into thick fog, and at the same time a short circuit put their wireless out of action. They reached the coast and turned southwards, but were compelled to make a forced landing in unfavourable conditions; their plane crashed, and turned upside down. They had covered 3,520 miles in forty-one hours—not bad, but no record.

Whilst this flight was proceeding, Jean Mermoz, a French flyer very well-known in South America, was on his way by ship from Rio de Janeiro to Bordeaux. He was responsible for establishing the airline service between Rio de Janeiro and Buenos Aires, flying day and night in all weathers. He had crashed and been stranded in the Great Cordillera, and his daring feats and his flying abilities had made him famous to such an extent that he was known as 'the French Lindbergh'. In fact, for a long time Mermoz had thought of trying the

Lindbergh feat in the other direction, from Paris to New York, but he had been unable to obtain the necessary backing and a suitable machine.

His mind was now on the South Atlantic. The non-stop crossing had been made, but he wanted to do better. He reckoned that the period of individual flights just for the glory of it was over, and he wanted to become known as 'the French Byrd' rather than 'the French Lindbergh'. Like Byrd, he was looking ahead to the days when big commercial airlines would maintain regular services over the routes that were now being flown for record-breaking purposes. In particular he had a regular weekly flight from Dakar (French West Africa) to Natal (Brazil) in mind, and it was on this that he now proposed to concentrate his efforts.

The first thing he needed was a suitable machine, and the Laté 28, a prototype built for the Aéropostale Lines, struck him as just right. Fully loaded, it could fly 2,500 miles non-stop. However, it would have to be made into a hydroplane, because for reasons of safety the French Government insisted that only hydroplanes should be used for long-distance flying over sea routes.

In March Mermoz obtained his licence as a pilot of air-transport hydroplanes, and on April 11th and 12th, as part of his training, he broke the duration record for hydroplanes. He decided to make his attempt during the full moon in the following May, and on May 12th an adapted Laté 28, named the *Comte de Vaulx*, was lying on the yellow waters of the River Senegal at St. Louis not far from Dakar, with 2½ cwt. of mail on board—the first transatlantic airmail. At 11.00 hours the engine started up; the hydroplane began to skim faster and faster over the surface of the river, and then took off like a bird—but a five-and-a-half-ton bird.

When Mermoz succeeded in getting that five and a half tons into the air on that first transatlantic mail flight, it was in some respects a more important day for aviation than many a more sensational but ephemeral feat. Thanks to Mermoz the air crossing of the Atlantic was now well on the way out of its uncertain beginnings. Henceforth it would be a regular every-day mail and transport service. But for the moment he was faced with all the same old difficulties: mechanical failures, bad flying weather, and, on this particular route, the doldrums, where the trade winds neutralize each other and there are constant tropical storms of great violence.

Mermoz himself was at the controls. He proposed to nurse his engine, and not ask too much of it in the first stages of the flight. His navigator, Dabry, checked the course regularly, and his wireless operator, Gimié, kept in touch with land-based wireless stations and with the two Aéropostale Line weather vessels, the *Phocée* and the *Brentivy*, which were posted on the route six hundred miles from the African and the South American coasts respectively.

The *Comte de Vaulx* was flying steadily at 100 miles per hour at low altitudes, varying according to circumstances from 250 feet to 650 feet above sea level. Below her the sea was calm and moving slowly in long, green undulations. 'I must confess that my heart was bounding with joy,' admitted Mermoz afterwards. At dusk they passed over the *Phocée*, lying motionless on a sea that was now dark violet. Mermoz brought down the plane to salute her. The crew of the *Phocée* assembled on deck to wave and cheer them on, saw the hydro-plane rise again into the red sky and fly on until it became a mere speck and finally disappeared.

'Look at that lot in the south-west,' said one of the sailors to his mates. It was grey and heavy, almost like lead. 'They're flying right into the doldrums.'

Mermoz had decided that he wanted a direct service to Natal, and for that he would have to fly through the notorious doldrums, but when he saw what was ahead of him he began to wonder whether perhaps he had not under-estimated the danger. They were flying straight towards a great wall of cloud which seemed to stretch higher and higher as they approached it. The clouds were unusually dense, and in constant movement, rolling and twisting and sweeping upwards without a moment's pause.

Well, he had met difficulties before. He judged the height of the cloud mass to be between thirteen and sixteen thousand feet, so it was no use thinking of flying over it; the hydroplane just hadn't the necessary ceiling. He would have to go through it. He brought the plane down to within 160 feet of sea level in the belief that he would find it easier to pass below rather than through the clouds. His judgment proved to be correct. Between two sombre masses to the east he thought he could distinguish a ray of light, the light of the moon shining over the doldrums.

And then it was as though a second night descended over the first, a night whose darkness was composed of vapour which was not exactly warm but of a suffocating tepidity which filled the lungs and enveloped the body like an intangible octopus. The corridor through which they were passing grew narrower until it was no more than a crevice, in which you could recognize the presence of light only because the darkness was not quite so dense. With tight lips Mermoz took his machine through it; his wing tips were invisible in the swirling cloud on either side. The pressure was so great now that water condensed everywhere inside the cabin, dripping from the instrument panel, soaking the maps, and running down the naked torsos of the airmen.

'Are you still in touch with land and sea stations, Gimié?' Mermoz asked.

'No, unfortunately I'm not.'

'Why's that?'

'Magnetic storms are causing interference. I can't make out a thing.'

Mermoz shrugged his shoulders. After all, what did it matter? If they got into trouble, no one could help them anyway. He had heard sailors in Brazil and West Africa talk about the doldrums as something terrible, a sort of marine hell, but he hadn't taken much notice. He could see what they meant now. Moreover, it could hardly be so bad on board ship as it was in this fragile bird-cage being pitched and tossed around. To make matters worse the engine wasn't taking too kindly to being soaked, and it was beginning to knock now and again.

'If the engine only holds we'll get through,' thought Mermoz, 'but if it doesn't . . .' His eyes were glued on that faint light of the May moon ahead of him towards which he was making as to a haven. The ordeal had lasted three hours now, and they were still not through; three hours in which he had had to keep on the alert the whole time, never relaxing for one moment, exchanging a word with his companions now and again, more to reassure them than anything else.

Then his attention was suddenly drawn to a vague light in the north-west. Was it an electrical phenomenon? It might be, of course. On the other hand it might be a break in this wretched blanket of cloud and vapour which was stifling them.

But even if it were a break it was not on his course. On the other hand, it might be worth while to take it in the hope that he could go round the worst of the doldrums after all. The thing was getting impossible. He made a few rapid calculations. To turn to the north-west now would mean a détour of something like sixty miles. He had enough fuel to allow for that, and he decided to take the chance.

The hydroplane was surging through the vapour at about 160 feet above the ink-like surface of the sea, and Mermoz changed course towards the north-west. After a while the three men had the impression that the sea below them was beginning to come to life again, whilst the clouds left and right seemed to be thinning. Gradually the cabin itself became lighter, revealing their tired and drawn faces.

And then suddenly it was all over, and the light of the moon shone down on a sea of silver; the clouds were gone and the stars were visible in the sky. Mermoz and his companions felt tremendous relief at their deliverance, and then a feeling of exaltation surged up.

'I feel like a horse let loose in a field,' exclaimed Mermoz. 'I feel I want to run, and jump, and turn cartwheels.'

'You'd better not do it here,' said Dabry drily. 'I've just picked up our position from the *Brentivy*. Here it is. We're O.K.'

Mermoz calmed down. It was quite true: better not do it here. They were men establishing a regular service, and were not out for a joy-ride.

'They're asking where we are,' said Dabry, shouting to make himself heard above the noise of the engine.

'Haven't you been sending out our position then?'

'Of course I have; every quarter of an hour. But some time ago I discovered that the aerial had been torn away by the storm. I've rigged up another one now, and it's all right again. You'd better have something to eat.'

He handed over sandwiches, two bananas and a bottle of champagne. At the welcome sight Mermoz realized that he was hungry and thirsty; that experience had taken it out of him, and the inner man needed sustenance.

He was tremendously confident now, but he did not allow his attention to relax; the flight was not over yet, and he checked his course with the information provided by the *Brentivy*, which was riding at anchor at St. Paul Rocks, hidden from sight by a layer of mist. They were making for Fernando Noronha through a sky full of squalls, but that bothered him very little after what they had been through in the doldrums.

'There should be about another hour to go,' said Dabry.

It passed in silence apart from the steady roar of the engine, and then in the distance a black point appeared on the horizon.

'My stomach contracted, and I felt my heart give a bound,' wrote Mermoz afterwards. 'I was so overcome it was almost as though my soul left my body, and I seemed numbed for the moment.'

'Saint Roque Cape!' exclaimed Dabry.

They had done it. There was the coast of Brazil, a tangible sign of their victory. They had flown 1,970 miles in 21 hours.

Not only had they carried out the first air-mail crossing of the South Atlantic, but they had broken the long-distance record for hydroplanes.

They came down on the yellow surface of the Rio Potengi, sending great sheafs of water swishing into the air. Mermoz shut off the engine. He was already thinking of the return journey.

A month later Mermoz climbed once again into the cockpit of his Laté 28. In the meantime the post had been carried to its various destinations in Rio, Montevideo, Buenos Aires and Santiago de Chile; Mermoz and his companions had been officially welcomed and fêted at receptions and banquets. He was glad to get back to work again, feel the controls in his hands, see the instrument panel in front of him, and whiff the smell of petrol in his nostrils.

It was night, and the moon was up, but unfortunately the wind was in the south-east, and the Rio Potengi was not wide enough to allow him to take off into the wind. Mermoz started up the engine, and the propeller began to turn. Then the *Comte de Vaulx* moved off, gathering speed, her floats leaving long glistening wakes behind on the surface of the river. The parallel wakes grew longer and longer . . .

'She's not coming off this time,' said Dabry.

And despite the full power of the engine and all the experience of Mermoz, it proved impossible to lift the $5\frac{1}{2}$ tons off the water. Mermoz shut off the engine and sighed. He certainly had no intention of giving up the attempt and waiting for more favourable conditions. He had done one crossing—the more difficult east–west one—successfully, but he was not primarily interested in that; he wanted to finish the job, and to make the return journey under whatever conditions afforded, thus proving that a regular weekly air-mail service between Europe and South America was a practical possibility.

'We'll just go on trying until we do get off,' he said.

He tried again and again, taking as much advantage of the

'Why's that?'

'It's a good sign. We're too near. We ought to spot her at any moment.'

And he was right: a minute or two later all three cried in unison: 'There she is!'

Mermoz brought the hydroplane down, and not a moment too soon, for the engine was boiling. The *Comte de Vaulx* skimmed the surface of the sea; as soon as the aircraft was sighted on board the *Phocée* a lifeboat was launched, for the crew had been told by wireless to be prepared to come to the hydroplane's assistance. Mermoz succeeded in putting his machine down safely in the trough between two waves, and lifeboat pulled towards them, see-sawing up and down in the rough sea.

When the boat came near enough they threw the mailbags into it, and after several attempts they managed to climb in themselves and were rowed back to the *Phocée* through the shark-infested sea. On board Mermoz began to discuss the possibilities of saving the *Comte de Vaulx*, but then rough seas smashed one of her floats; she tipped over sideways, and slid under the surface of the water.

The enormous difficulties he had experienced with the hydroplane take-off, difficulties which were likely to be repeated as soon as weather conditions were a little unfavourable, convinced Mermoz that weight for weight an ordinary plane was better for transatlantic flights. In any case, a hydroplane would not stay afloat for long in a rough sea, and this quite cancelled out its usefulness. He began to look around for a suitable machine, and he found it in a three-engined machine developing 2,000 h.p., designed by a thirty-year-old aero-engineer named Couzinet.

On January 16th, 1933, he flew from St. Louis to Natal in this machine, the *Arc-en-Ciel*, with a crew of four, taking Couzinet as a passenger—landing safely at Natal, and flying on afterwards to Rio de Janeiro and Buenos Aires. A few months later, on May 15th, he took off from Natal at three in the morning with the same machine to attempt the west–east crossing of the South Atlantic which he had tried unsuccessfully three years previously with the *Comte de Vaulx*. In the *Arc-en-Ciel* they now flew towards Africa at over 140 miles per hour, passing St. Paul Rocks in darkness, and then Fernando Noronha, and spotting the lights of a number of ships on the way.

The three engines were all running sweetly, and from time to time Mermoz checked them with his mechanic Collenot, the man who had been with him on his great Cordillera adventure. Already they had spotted and rectified a leak in the port engine, a mishap which would have proved fatal on the *Comte de Vaulx*. They were already sixty miles or so beyond the spot where the hydroplane had gone under, and they had another four hundred miles or so to go—about three hours' flying time. Mermoz reckoned that they would be in Dakar in good time for dinner.

But then the port engine began giving trouble again, and started to overheat dangerously. Collenot disappeared in the engine pit to see what could be done, and when he climbed out he was quite dazed.

'There's nothing to be done with her,' he gasped.

Mermoz shut off the troublesome engine, and his face darkened. If Collenot said there was nothing to be done, then there really was nothing to be done. It seemed very doubtful whether they would be in Dakar in time for dinner now. Fate seemed still determined that he should not fly the South Atlantic in the west–east direction. First the *Comte de Vaulx* had failed, and now apparently the *Arc-en-Ciel*. This time, too, they might not be so lucky. He throttled back the starboard engine. Fortunately the central engine was still running sweetly and producing sufficient power to keep the plane on her course, though their height was diminishing.

The others were well aware of the trouble, and they watched Mermoz at the controls as he sought to keep the plane on course and in the air. Messages describing the trouble were sent out; all ships were alerted, and destroyers hurriedly put out from Dakar. The most prudent thing, of course, would be to go down as soon as they sighted a ship, but Mermoz was determined to keep the plane in the air and on her course as long as possible. His resolution was rewarded. The *Arc-en-Ciel* showed what she could do in unfavourable circumstances: she stayed in the air and flew on—at no great height and at no great speed, but nevertheless she did fly on. It was dark when they spotted the first faint spark of light in the distance. It was on land, and soon they could see others. Mermoz began to smile, and his face relaxed—they were the lights of Dakar.

Fifteen minutes later he landed safely on the airfield, to be welcomed enthusiastically by a large crowd which had been waiting anxiously for the *Arc-en-Ciel* and intently following its struggle as the news was relayed over the wireless. This time Mermoz had done it.

A successful start had been made, and in 1934 the *Arc-en-Ciel* and her sister plane the *Croix du Sud* made twelve regular, commercial crossings of the South Atlantic. In the following year there were three times as many, and then the German Lufthansa appeared on the scene with a regular South Atlantic hydroplane service, whilst Dr. Eckener's Zeppelin also inaugurated a regular service.

In the meantime Mermoz himself had become a director of Air France, and he closely watched the development of what with a very good show of reason he could regard as his own particular line, occasionally taking the controls himself. On December 7th, 1936, he was engaged on such a flight—in the *Croix du Sud* this time. During the flight a brief message was received to the effect that the port engine had failed. The *Croix du Sud* did not arrive at her destination, and a very thorough search produced no result. Jean Mermoz had gone to his death in the South Atlantic. Another pioneer in man's fight to conquer the air over the oceans had become a victim.

11

An Unforeseen Danger

'THEY'RE going to crash!'

There seemed every justification for the excited exclamation. After scudding along the ground for well over a mile the plane had at last taken off, but slowly and heavily. As they watched, the pilot had not been able to get it high enough to straighten her out; her tail was still at a dangerous angle to the earth. The watchers fell silent, staring anxiously. As the plane failed to gain height their hearts were in their mouths, for at the end of the strand which had been used as a runway was a sea wall perhaps fifty feet high.

Fists were clenched now, and one or two of the spectators could not prevent themselves from crying out uselessly as though to warn the men in the plane—those Frenchmen who had tried so hard and so patiently and who deserved success. But now . . .

Inside the plane her crew of three—Assolant, Lefèvre and Lotti—needed no warning: they could see the danger for themselves. That wall there threatened to put an end—a ridiculous, silly end—to the patient work of a year during which they had made very possible preparation for their flight across the Atlantic on board their plane, the *Oiseau Canari*.

It was in 1928. Lotti was a dedicated flyer, and he was very keen on attempting a transatlantic flight. He approached Assolant, who was soon no less enthusiastic about the project. On September 2nd, 1928, with Lefèvre as their navigator, they set off, but owing to a series of mishaps they got no farther than Casablanca and had to turn back. By that time it was too late to think of trying again until the following year.

In 1929 they found themselves faced with an unexpected difficulty: the authorities temporarily prohibited all transatlantic flights—'particularly as in your case you would have a great deal of difficulty in getting the plane off the ground at all with the great weight of petrol you would need,' explained the government experts. The three flyers protested indignantly, but to no purpose.

'We won't let that stop us,' declared Lotti with determination.

'What do you mean?' demanded the other two. 'If they won't let us . . .'

'If they won't let us we'll fly from the States, that's all,' said Lotti resolutely. 'I've got a plan which I think will work. At least we can try it.'

One morning the three men presented themselves at Ourly aerodrome and asked permission to make a trial flight. Permission was given, and the plane took off—but long after its fuel must have been exhausted it had not returned. At first it was feared that the flyers had met with an accident, but then a message came that they had landed in England, at Southampton, where the plane was dismantled and taken on board the liner *Leviathan* for transport to New York.

In order to fly the Atlantic—or attempt to do so—they had been compelled to slip out of their own country like guilty men escaping from the police. But in their minds they could see themselves in a very different light when they returned— by air from the States.

They decided to take off on their transatlantic flight not from Roosevelt Field, but from the strand at Old Orchard, about 280 miles from New York. They made their first attempt with their plane, the *Oiseau Canari* on May 29th, 1929. They took off successfully, but it soon became evident that the mixture they were using was too light and was causing self-ignition, so that they had to turn back. By the time they were ready to take off again the weather conditions had worsened, and they had to wait for more favourable forecasts.

Lotti had been in New York, and he hurried back to Old Orchard on June 12th with the good news that an improvement in the weather, if only temporary, was promised for the following day. That night they tanked up the *Oiseau Canari* with not far short of 900 gallons of petrol, enough to keep her in the air for thirty-six hours. The plane was wheeled down from the dry sand to the damp, compact stretch nearer the sea, and at 10.00 hours the following morning the engine was started up and let run for a while; then Assolant made a trial take-off which was completely successful. But when he tried to take her off on the real thing, the inexplicable happened. The weight was the same; everything seemed the same, but for some reason the plane behaved as though it were much heavier, and try as he would Assolant could hardly get her to lift her tail to the horizontal position for the take-off. In the meantime she had gone much farther than on her previous take-off—and that sea wall was coming unpleasantly close.

Behind on the strand the watchers were flabbergasted, particularly the mechanic Leroy, the man who had been responsible for giving the *Oiseau Canari* her last check. What on earth could have gone wrong? The three flyers in their cabin were asking themselves the same thing. The weight had been most carefully calculated, everything had been reduced to a strict minimum, and all extra weight had been avoided—even their thermos flasks had been specially chosen for their lightness. During the trials with a full load the plane had been perfectly balanced, but now her tail seemed glued to the sands. And that sea wall was coming closer and closer . . .

Assolant, who was at the controls, was sweating like a bull as he used all his strength to pull back the control column, with Lefèvre helping him. 'Something like fifty feet,' he thought, 'and we're not even off the ground yet!' The throttle was full open and the engine was developing its full 600 h.p., but still the plane did not rise. Farther back in the cabin Lotti was at the emergency valve ready to jettison part of the petrol in order to let the plane rise, but he hesitated to operate the lever, for once he pulled it the flight would have to be abandoned, and he was prepared to do it only at the very last moment. That very last moment looked very near now, and still Assolant gave no order. He too seemed determined to leave it right to the last. And then Lotti realized that it was too late anyway. That sea wall was not much more than a hundred yards ahead. Unless the plane took off at once and gained height rapidly they would crash into the wall and end like a blazing torch.

When they were little more than sixty yards from the wall the miracle happened; the *Oiseau Canari* rose into the air, and instead of being straight ahead that wall was beneath her wings. The three men gasped in relief and relaxed. The *Oiseau Canari* had obeyed the controls in the nick of time. Below them was the surface of the sea. Assolant, who was breathing more easily now, swung the plane round in a great circle and flew over the strand again where the crowd of watchers was shouting and waving and jumping up and down in excitement and relief, and then the *Oiseau Canari* turned on to her course.

'A lucky escape,' said Lefèvre. Assolant grinned, but made no reply. There was nothing to add to that understatement. In any case, their troubles were obviously not over yet. For one thing they had lost height, and for another he didn't feel in full control of the plane; she was not answering well, and he was finding it difficult to keep her on course. Fortunately at least the weather was favourable. How would she be likely to behave in bad weather, perhaps with squalls of wind and rain? He preferred not to think about it.

'She's labouring a bit,' he said to Lefèvre. 'I'm afraid we'll have to lighten her.'

The one thing they couldn't spare, of course, was fuel, but there was Lotti's wireless set; that was the heaviest single item. They had relied on that to keep them in touch with the world during their flight, and to get their position. Lotti sorrowfully realized that if anything had to go it must be his wireless.

'We'll leave the decision for a while,' said Assolant. 'Perhaps she'll behave better as we go along.'

He was disappointed. They had prepared this flight so carefully, neglecting no detail however small; yet now, after all, something seemed to have gone wrong. You could do what you liked, and still you were at the mercy of imponderables—things over which you had no control whatever. Why had the take-off been so difficult? Another few moments and failure would have cost them their lives. And why was the *Oiseau Canari* answering so sluggishly to the controls? Why was it so difficult to keep her on course? Everything had been checked; everything had been gone into; and during their numerous trials she had behaved perfectly. Even now the engine was running smoothly enough, and the controls themselves seemed to be working properly; so why was the response so unsatisfactory? 'It's starting badly,' he thought, but he refused to consider turning back.

In the meantime Lotti was systematically dismantling his wireless apparatus. It was a pity, but if something had to go then obviously this must be it—if only the sacrifice would do the trick! He finished his preparations and then waited for an order from Assolant to ditch the apparatus. He could see only the back of Assolant's head as he sat there with Lefèvre at his side. Then he felt a hand on his shoulder, and turned with a start, quite ready to disbelieve the evidence of his senses. Involuntarily he gave an exclamation. And Lefèvre turned round to see what had happened.

There was a fourth man in the compartment, dragging himself up with difficulty out of the tail. All you could see at first was his head and shoulders, and then a long body as he pulled himself up. Assolant was looking round now too, and for a moment they were all too flabbergasted to utter a word.

'My name's Arthur Schreiber,' the apparition said, 'and I want to fly over the Atlantic with you.'

And then Assolant realized that the plane had recovered its normal buoyancy and was answering the controls easily. The whole thing was clear. The stowaway had been in the tail of the plane, completely upsetting its stability. It was a marvel that they could fly at all; and as for the take-off—that had been a miracle.

'God damn and blast you,' shouted Lefèvre, who was the first to find his tongue. 'You don't think you can get away with that.'

'Throw him into the sea,' shouted Assolant furiously. 'Four's too many. He nearly killed us all anyway.'

Arthur Schreiber, a young man of twenty, stood there with a white face and let the storm burst over him. It was a very difficult situation for the three flyers. The equilibrium of the *Oiseau Canari* was now restored, but the presence of the extra man meant a heavier weight and a greater fuel consumption— after they had cut everything down to the bone, and almost sacrificed their wireless! If they happened to run into bad weather and headwinds then the weight of the extra man might well tip the balance against them.

They glared at him with impotent fury, and tried to come to some decision. Of course they couldn't throw him overboard, though it was difficult to feel that he didn't deserve it. Should they turn back? That was clearly the most prudent solution. But then it would mean starting all over again; perhaps waiting endlessly for suitable weather, perhaps the failure of the whole undertaking. There was no real guarantee that once they had got rid of Schreiber they would be able to start again. They had already waited three weeks for the present improvement in the weather, and they had been warned that it was purely temporary. Further, their American rivals Williams and Yancey had been at Old Orchard with their plane the *Green Flash* preparing to leave immediately after them. They were presumably in the air already, and if the *Oiseau Canari* turned back now it would leave the field—and the favourable weather —to them. Moreover, if they turned back there would certainly be evil tongues wagging and saying that the stowaway had been merely a welcome excuse to abandon a dangerous flight. . . .

'Can you fly a plane, at least?' Assolant demanded unwillingly.

The fellow shook his head, and confessed that he didn't know the first thing about it. He was just a sensation seeker—a dead weight, a complete handicap, a minus quantity, something which greatly decreased their chances of success and endangered all their lives. It was infuriating.

Lotti remembered having been approached by the fellow with a ridiculous request that they should take him along with them. Lotti had smiled, patted him on the back and explained that it was impossible. But here he was after all, and Lotti didn't feel like smiling now.

'Do you realize what you've done?' he demanded. 'You nearly killed us all, and smashed our machine at the take-off because you upset the equilibrium; and the danger's not over yet. Your being here puts all our lives in peril. This isn't a liner where one passenger more or less doesn't matter.'

'The point is,' put in Lefèvre, 'what are we going to do with him now?'

'I'd very much like to throw him overboard,' said Assolant grimly, 'but we can't do that, and therefore we can't do anything for the moment. I'm not going back on his account. We'll keep on—and settle accounts with him later.'

'That blasted lout!' It was perhaps the tenth time that Assolant had uttered that heartfelt but impotent imprecation. Despite all his efforts, despite all his experience, he was unable to get the *Oiseau Canari* above 6,500 feet and out of the thick mist which swaddled and blinded them.

'Make the best progress you possibly can,' Kimball, the U.S. weather expert had advised him. 'There's a depression over Newfoundland and it's slowly moving southward. You want to get far enough out to miss it when it comes down; otherwise you're liable to run into trouble.'

Two hours after the take-off the forests of Nova Scotia had rolled away under the wings of the *Oiseau Canari*, and the visibility had been all right then, but in the distance to both right and left there were banks of menacing clouds and a north-west wind.

'All goes well. Everyone on board confident of success,' Lotti wirelessed.

And that was true; even the unexpected discovery of the stowaway had not robbed them of their confidence. They had calmed down now, and they still had the feeling that they could succeed in the great adventure and be the first Frenchmen to fly over the Atlantic in a French machine. Things did go quite well, too—until nightfall, and by that time the threat of deteriorating weather had become more tangible. The *Oiseau Canari* began to pitch and roll in the darkness, a darkness which was so intense that they could not see the tips of their wings and there was no longer sea or sky.

During the night the *Oiseau Canari* ploughed its way on through a violent storm which sometimes carried it perhaps a thousand feet higher into the air, and sometimes forced it down equally violently amidst a creaking and groaning which could be heard even above the noise of the storm. The altimeter needle oscillated violently, and whilst his companions held on tightly in the pitching, tossing plane, Assolant, his face streaming with sweat, worked grimly to keep the plane level and on her course and to gain altitude. At each new failure he would curse the presence of the reckless stowaway who was causing all the trouble.

'Am I on course?' he asked Lefèvre.

'I don't know,' came the unexpected reply.

'Why not? What's the matter?'

'The compass has taken leave of its senses. It's turning in all directions like a teetotum.'

'My God!' exclaimed Assolant, 'that's all we needed!'

The flight was a nightmare now, and worse than anything they had imagined. Assolant was flying a blind plane without a compass, a plane which was too heavily loaded to gain height.

'Are you in touch with shipping, Lotti?'

Lotti tried again, but without success.

'It's this magnetic storm,' he declared. 'It's ruining both transmission and reception.'

'We may be drifting off our course,' said Lefèvre.

Assolant shrugged his shoulders.

'If I can keep her out of the water I'll be satisfied,' he said. 'And it takes aerobatics to do that. If I put up this performance at an air display they'd be cheering like mad.'

The white-faced stowaway sat hunched up silently, probably regretting his stupid prank. He couldn't understand what the Frenchmen said to each other, but it was easy enough to see that the plane was in difficulties. He touched Lotti's arm. 'Are we in danger?' he asked timidly.

'You've said it,' said Lotti grimly. 'It's just a question of which lasts longest: this storm or our plane.'

'I've got a contact!' Lotti suddenly exclaimed. 'A ship, the *American Farmer*. Her W/T says the seas are very heavy.'

'Fancy that, now!' exclaimed Lefèvre ironically. 'Who'd have thought it!'

But a little later when he was staring out of the window northwards he shouted excitedly: 'A star! I can see a star. The cloud's breaking up.'

Everyone stared at the sky. It was not the first time that a star had brought men promise and hope. The clouds were certainly opening up towards the north, and at the same time the *Oiseau Canari* was steadier. No question about it: either the storm was declining or they were coming out of it on the other side. Lotti spotted the Pole Star and hurriedly seizing his sextant he got a sighting. After a quick calculation he declared that they had been driven southward off their course, as Lefèvre had feared.

'Perhaps instead of turning northward again we ought to make for the Azores,' he suggested. 'We could probably get out of the storm altogether that way.'

After a short discussion Assolant agreed with him, and within an hour they could see that they had done the right thing. It was much easier to fly the *Oiseau Canari*, and she was making much better progress.

'You can breathe again at last,' said Lotti appreciatively.

But not for long. The star disappeared, and the rough weather returned. The noise grew so loud they could no longer hear each other speak, and they communicated with each other by means of hurriedly scribbled messages. Lotti kept his headphones on all the time. Being in touch with other human beings on board ships sustained their morale and made them feel no longer alone. The receipt of messages from the outside world reduced the nervous tension in their own little world whose limits were otherwise so narrow.

'I've got the *Rochambeau*,' he announced gleefully.

The French liner congratulated them on their progress so far, sent them good wishes and gave them their position and the direction of the wind. After these were the *Laconia* and the *Niagara*, and then the stations on the Azores. At dawn they flew over the islands, the first land they had encountered since their departure from the New World. But they did not see it; the weather was too bad for that and the *Oiseau Canari* was still pitching and rolling.

'At least we're doing a regular 120 knots,' said Lefèvre. 'That's some consolation.'

They left the Azores behind them, after having been tempted for a moment or two to attempt a landing, which would, incidentally, not have been without its dangers. The grey dawn showed them their tired and drawn faces. It hadn't been an easy run so far, and no one had had a wink of sleep. Lefèvre was at the controls now and Assolant was sitting in Lefèvre's seat eating a sandwich and considering their situation. From the beginning he had left open the possibility of two routes: the one farther to the north, which was more or less the route taken by Lindbergh, and the other farther south, via the Azores. Fate had taken a hand, and it was the second course they were now following, which meant that the Spanish coast would be their first sight of Europe. He reckoned they ought to make it by the end of the day—between Oporto and Finisterre.

That wasn't too precise, and yet considering the difficulties they had surmounted, flying blind over long stretches, it wasn't too bad. Once again Assolant cursed the foolish lad who had spoiled all their plans and probably ruined their chances of landing in France.

When Assolant had finished his simple meal he took the controls again. The sky was still covered, and they had seen the Atlantic only two or three times since leaving Old Orchard. They hadn't sighted a single ship on the way, and that had been rather disappointing—not that it was of any practical import-ance, but it would have cheered them up. He smiled as he remembered an incident that had occurred during the night, at the worst period of their troubles.

Someone had glimpsed a light. A lighthouse? The naviga-tion lights of a ship? A searchlight? It didn't really matter what it was; it could be of no help to them. But somehow the thought that there were other men below them had encouraged and cheered them. They no longer felt so alone; that light winking there in the darkness had raised their spirits. And then they had realized that they were looking at a rising star. They had laughed at their own mistake, but that moment or two of illusion had acted like a tonic, and had not been altogether dissipated by their awakening.

'We shan't have enough fuel to take us all the way,' said Lefèvre. 'The best thing to do would be to land as soon as we find a suitable spot.'

From the late afternoon on they began to keep a lookout for land. Lefèvre had profited from a brief appearance of the sun to discover their position. They were consoled to find that their course was accurate; to sight Europe now meant not only victory, but sheer survival. At 17.00 hours they sighted a dark ridge ahead, and at first they thought it was land, but it turned out to be just a darker bank of cloud. Once again the sea beneath them was invisible.

'We could be over Spain already,' said Lefèvre.

It was just possible, and Assolant turned down the nose of the *Oiseau Canari* to find out, but it was the sea that came into view: a greyish green sea streaked with breakers, and stretching away endlessly in all directions. There was not a sight of land. Assolant took the plane higher again and they flew on. If they did not make landfall before darkness fell their situation would be unenviable.

'The sun must still be up,' said Lefèvre. This was true, but there wasn't a sign of it in the grey sky, which now seemed to be darkening. By 19.00 hours they were beginning to grow anxious. Not only did they need light to make a forced landing if they did reach Europe, but their fuel was running out now. They were not quite sure just how much they had left but they knew that it could not be a great deal, so to all their other troubles was gradually added the fear that at any moment the engine might begin to cough and splutter before finally giving up the ghost.

Lefèvre was studying the map, looking keenly at the coasts of Portugal and North-Western Spain, looking for some salient feature which would be easily recognizable. And then in the distance they sighted land!

At the first indication three more faces were glued to the look-out. There it was, a long, unmoving line beyond the moving surface of the sea. At last!

'That's Cape Finisterre!' shouted Lefèvre, and they hugged each other with joy—even the wretched Schreiber was not left out. Smiling with satisfaction Assolant flew along the coast looking for a suitable place to land, but it was a good hour before he found one, a length of flat sand big enough to take the plane and give it the necessary run to take off again. He brought down the *Oiseau Canari* and landed her without the slightest difficulty.

Assolant shut off the engine and the four men clambered to the ground in a silence which seemed absolute, and it was only after a while that they began to distinguish noises; the soughing of the sea on the shore, the cries of gulls in the air—and then the sound of birds chirping. To the right of them a rotating light swung round in the gathering dusk. They had found a landing place not a moment too soon, having flown along the northern coastline of Spain almost as far as Santander. In all they had put 3,600 miles behind them in 28 hours and 52 minutes. Assolant heaved a great sigh of relief, for he had carried the greatest burden.

'That's that, at last,' he said.

12

Paris to New York at Last!

THE *Oiseau Canari* finally landed in Paris on June 14th, where Assolant, Lefèvre and Lotti were welcomed with tremendous enthusiasm. Their machine, which had left France in secrecy only two months before, was now exhibited triumphantly at the Tuileries, and the French people were greatly cheered by the thought that the Atlantic had at last been flown by Frenchmen in a French machine. This was a great success, certainly, but in their hearts they still hoped for an even greater one: the direct flight from Paris to New York, which as yet no one had made, but for which Nungesser and Coli had given their lives.

Of course, there were already a good many French flyers with their eyes on that coveted honour, and amongst them the most likely seemed to be Costes, a flyer of great experience and sober judgment, a man who knew how to be patient when necessary. He had that flight well in mind, but he had no illusions about the extraordinary difficulties involved. Another great flyer, Commander Byrd, had declared two years previously that the east–west flight was vastly more difficult than the flight in the other direction, the one he had made himself. In the two years which had passed since then, aeronautics had, of course, made a certain amount of progress, and aeroplanes were available with higher performances, but that made very little difference to the fact that a flight would still largely depend for its success on meteorological conditions, because any flyers would have to reckon primarily with west–east winds for the greater part of the flight—and, so far at least, man was not in a position to control the weather. But it was a flight that Costes nevertheless proposed to undertake, and on July 13th an announcement raised new enthusiasm: Costes and Bellonte had taken off from Le Bourget at 5.30 that morning on their way to New York in a Bréguet plane called the *Point d'Interrogation*. Despite the enthusiasm aroused by the flight, the plane seemed well named.

Another couple of flyers were on the way too, with the same objective: New York. These were two Poles, Idzikovski and Kubala. These two had already tried once, during the previous year, but had run into engine trouble. That was bad luck, but at least they had had the good luck to be picked up alive and well by a German ship, having got as far as the Azores.

The first messages from Costes and Bellonte were optimistic: everything was going according to plan and they were making good progress. Then came a signal to say that they were about a hundred miles from the Azores. But at 18.15 hours another and unexpected message to say that they were turning back. Everyone wondered what had happened. It turned out to be the same old problem; they had met such strong head winds that their speed had been reduced to about fifty miles per hour. There was no knowing how long they would have to contend with such winds, and at that rate they might not have had sufficient fuel to take them to the other side, and certainly not enough to reach New York. Costes was unwilling to do anything but the full job he had set out to do, so the *Point d'Interrogation* put about, doing the return journey to Le Bourget, aided by the following winds, in record time. They landed after having flown 3,354 miles in 28 hours, no mean performance.

'As for New York,' said Costes laconically, 'it was a disappointment, of course—but, another day . . .'

In the meantime tragedy had overtaken the two Polish flyers. Once again they met with engine trouble and had to make a forced landing, this time in the Azores on Graciosa Island. Unfortunately they crashed, and the machine turned over. Kubala crawled out of the wreckage uninjured, but his companion Idzikovski was killed outright.

Costes gave up the New York flight project for that year, and on September 27th he took off on a non-stop long-distance flight eastward, landing in Manchuria after having flown 4,910 miles non-stop and broken the long-distance flying record.

The following year, 1930, Costes and Bellonte were ready again in the spring to attempt the flight from Paris to New York if a favourable opportunity afforded. Although they were very anxious indeed to be the first, Costes was quite determined to take no chances and to start the flight only if there were a reasonable hope of favourable weather—irrespective of what others might do.

There appeared to be no competitors for the east–west flight from Paris to New York, but on June 23rd a young Australian named Kingsford-Smith set off in his plane, the *Southern Cross*, from Ireland to make the east–west flight a second time from there, as the Germans von Huenefeld and Köhl, and the Irishman Fitzmaurice had already done. Kingsford-Smith was not without experience of long-distance flights; during the previous year he had been lost in the Australian bush, where he had made a forced landing after a Pacific flight, and it had been a week before he had been found. He had a crew of three with him on this transatlantic flight: Van Dyck, Saul and Stannage.

They fell in with very bad weather, and at times their plane was forced down so low that their underslung antenna was dragging in the water, but in the end they managed it and landed in Newfoundland, having been very lucky indeed to find a break in the clouds which enabled them to do so. They had covered the 2,000-odd miles from Ireland to Newfoundland in 31 hours and 30 minutes, which was no record; but at least they had made the east–west crossing for the second time and under conditions which would probably have meant disaster to a less experienced pilot.

On August 20th a German pilot, von Gronau, set off with his Dornier flying boat to explore the possibilities of the far northern route to America via Iceland and Greenland. The Dornier covered 4,250 miles in six stages, and was in the air a total of 44 hours and 15 minutes; a fine performance, but more or less outside the transatlantic rivalry.

Costes was still biding his time. He and Bellonte had made numerous successful trial flights with the *Point d'Interrogation*, which had a new engine of 780 h.p. With over a thousand gallons of fuel in the tanks they would have a non-stop range of 5,600 miles, which would give them a safety margin of about fifty per cent on the 3,600-mile journey. Bellonte, the navigator, had drawn up a detailed plan for the whole flight, setting out hour by hour the altitude, the fuel consumption, the mileage, and so on.

Twice a day Costes studied the meteorological charts for the Atlantic, and so far he had been compelled to decide against any attempt. This waiting had been going on for a couple of months now, and the summer would soon be ended, after which the chances of good weather would be even less. It was galling, but at the same time he was determined to take no chances—he didn't want a skin-of-the-teeth victory, as both the other east–west crossings had been; he wanted to make the much longer flight—Paris to New York—and make it properly and with a good margin to spare, a real conquest of the Atlantic. So far he had succeeded in doing everything he had set out to do, except this flight, and he was determined to succeed in that as well—and if he did succeed it would be for the same reason: he knew how to prepare thoroughly and wait patiently.

On August 30th things looked rather brighter. Ridges of high pressure promised stable weather over the Atlantic for a while. Admittedly there were two troughs of depression, one to the west of Ireland and the other between the Azores and Newfoundland, but even they were declining.

'And you can hope for easterly winds,' was the final encouraging remark.

On August 31st the *Point d'Interrogation* was made ready at Le Bourget, and Costes at last consented to tell the journalists his plans. His announcement was short and to the point: 'We shall take off for New York tomorrow morning.'

That night he gave the machine a last check-over, and left the mechanics tanking up by searchlight. Then he went home to get a few hours sleep. At midnight provisions were packed away on board: cold chicken, hot soup in thermos flasks, tinned stuff, and champagne. The number of shadows on the aerodrome began to increase. People were gathering to witness the start, and their numbers increased after the theatres and the night-clubs closed down. A number of personal friends of the flyers were there too, including Codos, who had assisted Costes in the preparations for the flight. 'The weather outlook is unusually good,' he announced. 'Costes has had courage enough to bide his time. He has every hope of succeeding now.' People looked up into the sky; it was clear and stars were twinkling, and a great searchlight beam swung round and round steadily.

At four o'clock in the morning Bellonte arrived, showing no signs of excitement. He chatted to the mechanics putting the last touches to the plane, which was standing ready on the runway. Officials of the Aero Club arrived to make the necessary checks for record purposes. The sky in the east gradually began to lighten, but the atmosphere no longer seemed so clear. 'Just a morning mist,' said someone. 'Nothing of any importance.'

As yet Costes himself had not appeared, and people began to wonder what had happened to him. 'He's gone to the Meteorological Office for a last-minute weather forecast,' someone said. There was a big crowd present now, and those who had gone to sleep were waking up as it grew lighter. There was a cheerful and festive atmosphere, with a good deal of laughter.

'It was different when Nungesser and Coli set off,' someone said. 'The atmosphere was much more tense; people hardly spoke above a whisper, and there were long silences—as though at a funeral.'

The memory caused those in the neighbourhood to fall silent for a moment or two. Three years ago Nungesser and Coli had tried and failed at the cost of their lives; perhaps these other two Frenchmen, Costes and Bellonte, would succeed now and turn disaster into triumph.

Suddenly there was a movement amongst the crowd, the sound of a car hooter, and shouts of: 'It's Costes'. Costes stepped out of the car, as calm as Bellonte, but smiling, as though he might have been going up for a pleasure trip. His wife was with him; she wore a costume to match the colour of his plane, and embroidered on her hat was a question mark. Costes shook hands with Bellonte.

'What's the latest weather forecast?' Bellonte asked.

'A bit rough until we get beyond Ireland, and then we ought to have the wind behind us.'

Bellonte seemed a little nervous now, and he looked pale.

'What about this stuff?' he asked, meaning the mist on the airfield, which was growing thicker. Favourable winds over the Atlantic and then perhaps be unable to take advantage of them because of a wretched ground mist in Paris!

'It won't stop us, Bellonte. We're going.'

Costes looked confident and he spoke confidently, but almost at once weather bulletins announced that visibility was down to ten per cent in a radius of 180 miles.

'We'll start,' he repeated—'even if we have to go on foot!' And he laughed.

But the time crept on. Codos went up on a reconnaissance flight. When he returned he was not optimistic.

'Pea soup as far as you can see,' he said.

Costes made his way towards where his car was standing.

'I'll be back,' he said shortly, and the car moved off. He decided on a last consultation with the weather experts. It didn't much matter what the weather was like at Le Bourget. He wanted to know whether there had been any change in the situation over the Atlantic in the meantime. If the forecasts were still favourable he would take off.

'No change,' they told him. 'There's still every likelihood of favourable winds.'

'What about this damned mist?'

'Localized in North-West France. And it will disperse.'

Costes got back into his car and returned to the airfield.

'Well?' demanded Bellonte anxiously.

'It's all right. We're going.'

Bellonte looked up. There was still thick mist.

'It's going to be all right,' Costes assured him. 'We shall have to wait a bit, that's all.'

And Costes calmly went into a hangar and stretched himself out on a camp-bed to get some more sleep. At half-past ten Codos woke him.

'I've been up again,' he said. 'It's clearing. I think you could do it all right now.'

'Fine!' exclaimed Costes, stretching himself. 'We will.'

The two flyers put on their flying kit, and went over to the *Point d'Interrogation* amidst the cheers of the crowd. Costes acknowledged them with a wave of the hand as he climbed into the cockpit followed by Bellonte.

'All ready?' asked Costes. Bellonte nodded.

'Right, then,' and Costes gave a sign to the waiting mechanic to swing the propeller. The engine started; and Costes let it run for a while to warm up, then he opened the throttle and it began to roar. Costes gave another sign and mechanics pulled away the chocks. The *Point d'Interrogation* began to roll forward, and thousands of eyes followed the red biplane as it increased speed along the runway. Six and a half tons, and it had to be lifted off the ground.

Thirty seconds after the start the watchers saw the tail rise until the plane was moving horizontally along the runway; a few seconds later the plane was off the ground. The take-off had been carried out in about thirteen hundred yards. It was a good start. But suddenly there were shouts of dismay from the watching crowd: the *Point d'Interrogation* had tipped sideways. Luckily it was nothing serious. Costes corrected it at once, and after flying low for another three hundred yards or so the plane gained height rapidly, turned to the north-west and disappeared into the mist escorted by half a dozen other planes.

A small plane crossed the route of the *Point d'Interrogation*, and its pilot waved farewell. Costes, who was at the controls, recognized his friend Codos and waved back. The smaller plane now made southwards and disappeared.

The *Point d'Interrogation* crossed the Oise and flew along the Seine Valley. Costes sighted Rouen, and they finally left the French coast at St. Valèry en Caux. An hour later they sighted Southampton to starboard. The weather had cleared considerably by this time, and they could see a big trawler putting out into the Atlantic, leaving a long white trail in the dark green sea. The Atlantic! The test had begun!

All ships steaming between Europe and America had been warned to keep a look-out for the *Point d'Interrogation*, and the weather ship *Jacques Cartier* was regularly transmitting the latest weather forecasts and giving the flyers all possible information likely to be of assistance to them. The first ship to get into touch with the *Point d'Interrogation* was the liner *Rochambeau*. That was at 17.30 hours, and at that time everything was in order. An hour later Bellonte sent out a message to say that they were being a good deal bothered by cloud, and that they were setting a north-west course.

At that time they were 500 miles out into the Atlantic and beginning to run into their first difficulties. Costes flew round a great cloud mass and Bellonte took a bearing on the sinking sun. Then he tried to get into touch with the *Rochambeau* again, but she was too far away. It was dark now, and the sea was invisible below them, but it was a clear starry night. From time to time Bellonte took a bearing on Arcturus or Aldebaran, checked their position and entered it on the route which he had so carefully mapped out. The sound of the engine was

regular and it was running quite smoothly at cruising speed.
There seemed no cause for apprehension at the moment.

Now and again the stars would disappear and they would
find themselves flying blind in complete darkness. But for the
quickly scribbled notes they exchanged from time to time,
each man, who could now see only the other's silhouette,
might have thought himself completely alone. During the
night they put mile after swift mile behind them, and down
below a number of ships were following their passage by
wireless: after the *Rochambeau* it was the big German liner, the
Bremen then the U.S. liner *America*, and the weather ship
Jacques Cartier. When dawn broke behind the *Point d'Interrogation* they were to the south-east of Newfoundland. A little later
they were off Miquelon. When they heard the plane's position
the various stations began to discuss its chances.

'They've put the worst part of the journey behind them.'

'The longest part perhaps, but not necessarily the worst.
They're entering a zone of fog and storm along the American
coast.'

'The greater part of their fuel load has been used now, and
the plane will be lighter and better able to cope.'

'That's true. On the other hand, both of them are probably
tired and perhaps numbed with cold.'

The messages picked up regularly during the course of the
morning were reassuring. Then from 12.30 hours onwards
nothing further was heard, although the stations on the
American coast were joining in now. Next the station at
Louisburg put out a heartening message: their wireless silence
could only be because of a fault in their apparatus; they were
all right, for they had been sighted shortly after midday.

That message was read with relief not unmixed with scep-
ticism, because people could remember all the hopeful but
false reports which had been issued in connection with the
Nungesser and Coli flight. Then this ill-concealed misgiving
was strengthened by reports of sightings in two different and
widely separated spots at the same time; they couldn't both be

true. Moreover, there was another cause for misgiving: Lindbergh, who had been staying with his mother, had set off to fly to New York to be present to welcome Costes and Bellonte when they arrived, and it seemed that his plane was lost in the fog, for nothing further had been heard of him.

Crowds of New Yorkers had gathered on and around Curtis Field to welcome the *Point d'Interrogation* just as crowds of Parisians had gathered at Le Bourget to welcome Lindbergh. They were enlivening the waiting time by spotting celebrities.

'There's Jean Borotra!'

'And that's Alain Gerbault.'

It so happened that quite a number of famous Frenchmen who were also well-known abroad were in New York at the time—Borotra, Gerbault, Doret and the famous boxer Georges Carpentier—and they were all on the airfield to welcome Costes and Bellonte on their arrival. The crowds were also on the look-out for Lindbergh, but he was nowhere to be seen. 'Any news of Lindy?' It was a question that was frequently asked, but no one was able to provide a satisfactory answer. And as for Costes and Bellonte, their plane was now reported to have been sighted over Old Orchard, in which case they wouldn't be very long.

At 16.30 hours there was a movement amongst the crowd, and shouts of 'They're coming!' Instinctively people searched the sky, but it was still empty. In fact the shouts referred to the arrival of a car with Lindbergh and his wife, and there were loud cheers. Lindbergh explained that heavy mist had compelled them to make a forced landing in Pennsylvania and come on by car.

'I wouldn't have missed being here for worlds,' he declared to the representative of the French Ambassador, Paul Claudel, who was unable to be present. 'What's the latest news of them?'

He was told of their wireless silence.

'It could easily be a breakdown of their transmitter,' he said optimistically. 'Really not enough to worry about. Costes is a fine pilot, and he's accomplishing a greater feat than I did.'

Lindbergh was nothing if not generous, and he was talking about the two Frenchmen as though they had already succeeded. His optimism proved to be well founded, and at 17.40 hours a report came in that the *Point d'Interrogation* had been sighted and recognized beyond all doubt, 145 miles from New York.

The French tricolour was flying over Curtis Field now, and the American Legion already had a guard of honour drawn up. At 18.45 hours cheering broke out and rose into a roar, but it was a false alarm; there was, as yet, still no sign of the French plane.

In Paris, where it was shortly before midnight at that time, a great crowd had assembled in the Place de la Concorde. Loudspeakers were relaying the latest news. The atmosphere was the same as in that earlier night from May 9th to May 10th, but this time the encouraging reports were accurate. There was no doubt whatever that the *Point d'Interrogation* had made the transatlantic crossing from east to west safely and was now flying down the American coast to New York. Then came an announcement that the French plane was an hour's flying time from New York, and that a squadron of seven U.S. planes was escorting it in.

All traffic had come to a standstill on the Place de la Concorde, and there was no sound of horns; cars had given up the attempt to get through. There was silence in the great square, and only the distant noise of Paris could be heard. Everyone was awaiting the voice from New York which would announce the arrival of the two French flyers; contact had already been established, and the reception was good.

At midnight the crowds on the Place de la Concorde could hear the noise of the crowds on Curtis Airfield through the loudspeakers. 'A few more minutes now,' announced a voice. And then suddenly they could hear the roar of plane engines growing louder and louder until they went under in a great shout of acclamation. Costes and Bellonte had done it! The east–west transatlantic crossing from Paris to New York had been achieved at last. The fond dream of years was a reality. Costes himself was brought to the microphone to say a few words to the crowds gathered on the Place de la Concorde, and then Bellonte spoke. When the two flyers had finished a band on the Curtis Airfield struck up the 'Marseillaise' and the music was relayed to the waiting crowd in Paris, who joined in with enthusiasm; a moving confirmation of man's victory over intervening space.

.13

Amelia Earhart

At 07.50 hours on June 19th, 1928, the look-out on board the U.S. liner *America* reported a plane flying in from the Atlantic towards the Irish coast at about 2,500 feet. Captain Friend, who was on the bridge, studied it through his glasses.

'A hydroplane,' he said. 'You can distinguish the long floats.'

'A naval reconnaissance plane, I expect,' said the officer of the watch.

At that moment the hydroplane, whose course cut diagonally across that of the *America*, turned and flew several circles over the liner.

'I wonder what they want?' said the Captain.

Then the stranger swooped low across the liner, and something dropped down. No doubt it had been intended for the liner's deck, but it fell into the sea, sending up a short spurt of water.

The officer of the watch laughed.

'They're dropping bombs now, sir,' he said.

The plane turned and came down again; again an object fell away from it, and again it fell into the sea, but closer to the liner this time.

'What did I tell you?' exclaimed the facetious officer. 'They're trying to sink us. They're getting the range too.'

Captain Friend shrugged his shoulders indulgently.

'They're obviously in high spirits this morning,' he said.

But he was wrong. The plane had turned away, but inside its cockpit the three flyers were in anything but high spirits: they had been hoping to discover their position from that liner. They had been flying across the Atlantic for hours, and they were lost. They had been unable to take their bearings, because the weather they had encountered had hidden the sun during the day and the stars at night. The sight of that liner steaming out of the mist had raised their hopes, but now they were dashed.

There were three of them in that cockpit: two men named Gordon and Schultz and a young woman, a certain Amelia Earhart. It was she who had dropped the messages—each weighted with an orange. She was mortified at her failure, and beginning to wonder how the adventure would end. She knew how it had begun—with a telephone call.

'You're wanted on the phone, Miss Earhart.'

The young woman, surrounded by orphan children in Denison House, the well-known social foundation in Boston, made a gesture of impatience.

'Say I'm engaged,' she said.

'I've already said that, Miss Earhart, but the gentleman won't take no for an answer. It's very important, he says.'

The young woman hesitated, then left the children and went to the telephone.

'Captain Reilly here,' said a voice. 'Tell me, Miss Earhart, would you like to undertake an important flying trip?'

'What sort of a flying trip?'

'One with a certain amount of risk and danger.'

'That wouldn't frighten me.'

'Good, I didn't think it would. I'd like to see you first though. Could you come and see me in my office this evening?'

'Very well.'

That evening the young woman went to Captain Reilly in his office, very curious to know what was behind the mysterious message. Captain Reilly lost no time in telling her.

'You know that no woman has yet flown across the Atlantic?'

'Of course.'

'Now one woman was intending to try, but for personal

reasons she has had to abandon her plans. But she would like someone to take her place—another American girl.'

For a moment Reilly said nothing, but just looked at his visitor.

'And the point is,' he went on, 'would you like to be that American girl?'

Amelia Earhart made no reply for a moment or two. The proposition took her breath away—it was beyond her wildest dreams. She was certainly keen on flying, and she was a member of several women's flying clubs, but she had never thought of doing anything outstanding—and as for flying the Atlantic . . .

'And the conditions?'

'It wouldn't cost you a cent. The lady I mentioned just now is Amy Phipps. She has bought a three-engined Fokker plane from Commander Byrd.'

'A three-engined plane!'

'Well, you wouldn't be on your own, of course. There'd be a pilot and a mechanic with you.'

'You mean I'd be just a passenger?'

'If you like to put it that way. But a passenger who would be risking just as much as the others.'

'I shouldn't like to be just a passenger. I'd like to pilot the plane part of the way at least.'

'I dare say that could be arranged.'

Once again Amelia Earhart fell silent for a moment or two whilst she considered the matter. A flight over the Atlantic was certainly a dangerous undertaking at the best of times, but think of the joy and triumph at being the first woman to do it!

'You can count on me,' she said simply.

'Fine. That's as far as we can get for the moment, because I must put the matter before my committee, but I think everything will go smoothly.'

Amelia Earhart carried on with her job without saying a word to anyone about the Atlantic flight possibility, though her mind busied itself with the project constantly. In her spare time she went frequently to look at the Fokker, which was now being turned into a hydroplane in preparation for the flight. She had already made the acquaintance of the two men she was to fly with: Bill Schultz, the pilot, and Lou Gordon, the mechanic.

'The end of May, we reckon,' Bill told her.

Amelia Earhart made one or two trial take-offs and flights with the two men. On June 2nd, the orange and gold Fokker, now a hydroplane, and named *Friendship*, took off from Boston and touched down in Trepassey Bay, Newfoundland, the point from which their transatlantic crossing was to start.

'All we need now is a favourable weather forecast,' said Bill, 'but we may have to wait for that. It may be tomorrow; it may be next month.'

Actually they had to wait twelve days, and it seemed more like twelve weeks. Every morning the New York Weather Bureau provided them with the latest forecasts, and they kept an eye on the local wind on their own account. They needed a south-east wind for the take-off, but the trouble was that south-east winds often brought heavy mist with them; and that wasn't so good, particularly as they tended to hang about for a long time at sea. Once or twice Bill Schultz actually started, but each time he returned to their starting point—the visibility had been really too bad.

On June 17th they climbed into the cabin of the Fokker once more. Whilst not being ideal for their purposes, the latest weather forecasts were not too bad.

'We'll have to put up with it,' said Bill Schultz. 'We've hung around quite long enough for my liking. If I can get her into the air we'll go. Fifty miles per hour would do me, I think.'

He taxied the plane to the back of the harbour and then turned her nose seaward. The engines were running at full pitch now, and she began her run. Amelia Earhart's eyes were glued to the speedometer. The needle was oscillating between thirty and forty: not good enough. The floats were sending up sheaths of water into the air and the machine was almost lost in spray.

'Fifty!' she exclaimed.

Schultz opened her at full throttle.

'Fifty-five, sixty,' counted Amelia.

Then two of the three engines began to splutter. If they lost power now there would be no hope of getting the heavily laden machine into the air. At the controls Schultz was working desperately to get her off the water. She rose for a moment or two and then dropped back, sending a tremendous wave into the air, but then she rose again. She was flying now, actually in the air, though only few feet above the surface. Then slowly and steadily the *Friendship* gained height.

'We're off,' said Schultz exultantly. 'I thought we weren't going to do it when those two engines started to splutter. There was nothing wrong with them, luckily; it was just the bath they were getting. As long as the salt doesn't cake the plugs!'

The mist brought up by the south-east wind swallowed the *Friendship* for a while, let her go, and then closed in again. Schultz took the *Friendship* up into the clear air above, but down below all sight of the sea was cut off by a waste of billowing mist.

Amelia sat looking out with interest. The changing shapes of the clouds and the mist fascinated her, and from time to time she made an entry in the log. At 20.00 hours Lou Gordon, who was also operating the wireless transmitter, took off his headphones and leant back with an exclamation.

'Are we on course?' demanded Schultz.

'That's just what I'd very much like to know.'

'What do you mean? Can't you get our position from ships?'

'That's just it; I can't. The radio's broken down. Can't get a thing out of it. Can't send; can't receive either. From now on we're out on our own, brother and sister.'

When they left the *America* behind in the mist, Amelia Earhart, Bill Schultz and Lou Gordon held a council of war. They were quite sure from the distance they had already covered that land could not be far off, but the thing that really puzzled them was the course being steamed by the *America*—instead of being in line with their own there was a quite considerable divergence. Was their own course wrong? Did it mean that if they continued along it they might miss the Irish coast? The mist was growing thicker; it was practically fog now. Through it they sighted the looming shapes of vessels from time to time, but they were only fishing trawlers.

'Let's hope a few of them will be around when we have to go down,' said Gordon, 'because we've got about enough fuel for another hour, not more.'

They needed to spot land before that though if they were to land safely. In the meantime every break in the mist showed them nothing but endless green sea with an occasional fishing trawler.

'They're quite small,' said Schultz hopefully. 'They're not likely to venture very far from the shore. We must be fairly close to land.'

But even if that were true it wouldn't necessarily help them much; if they were off course they might spend their precious fuel flying along parallel to the coast and never reaching it. What could they do? Alter course on a hunch? Schultz didn't feel justified in following his own instinct in the matter; after all, he had no real reason for his feeling. No, the best thing was to carry on as before.

'More cloud,' said Amelia.

There was rain too now, and the cabin windows of the *Friendship* were being slashed with it. The weather was deteriorating, and the horizon was as heavy as lead. Schultz took the plane up higher in order to get above the clouds, but the engine began to splutter, stopped for a moment or two, started up again. Their hearts were in their mouths, but the engine resumed its normal smooth running.

'I thought that was it,' said Schultz. 'The tank must be nearly empty. The engine was getting fuel only in the horizontal position; as soon as I put her nose up the fuel rushed back and no longer reached the feed-pipes. Which means we can't get up. We'll just have to stay in this soup.'

But then, not more than a mile or so away, they saw a coastline, a coast with cliffs broken here and there, and behind them they could see trees, green pastures and roads. They completely failed to recognize it—and no wonder, for it was not Ireland, as they expected, but Wales.

They crossed the coast inland, swung around and flew along it for a while, until they came across a small town and a little port. Schultz put down the nose of the *Friendship* and touched down easily on the surface of the harbour, watched from the quay by groups of not particularly excited Welshmen, who did not as yet know that the hydroplane had flown the Atlantic and that the first woman ever to do so was on board.

'In short, for all her part in the flight Amelia Earhart might have been a parcel.'

Amelia Earhart was a modest young woman, and she made no objection to this rather discourteous description of her feat by a snooty journalist. Although it had originally been intended that she should pilot the *Friendship* some part of the way, the weather throughout the crossing had in fact been so bad that Schultz had not felt himself justified in handing over the controls to her at any time. Others were more generous to the first woman to fly across the Atlantic, and she was fêted and honoured, and her courage lauded. But Amelia Earhart was not altogether satisfied; she wanted to fly the Atlantic and do it on her own; and she swore inwardly that one day she would do something to earn the plaudits which were now being showered on her.

She therefore set herself to gain the necessary experience, and she flew more and more often, for longer and longer periods, even setting up a number of new records. In 1932 she decided that she was ready to tackle the task she had set her-self: to fly the Atlantic on her own. She proposed to start if possible on the anniversary of Lindbergh's take-off for Paris, but unfortunately the weather at the time was too bad to allow her that little symbolism, and according to the weather experts no improvement was to be expected for several days. How-ever, on May 20th the weather unexpectedly improved. A day or so later Amelia decided to start, and on May 22nd at 19.12 hours her plane, a Lockheed Vega, took off from Harbour Grace.

Three hours after she had left land behind her the moon rose from behind a bank of fleecy clouds, and once again she felt the elation she had experienced on that first flight over the Atlantic between sea and sky; the magic of the unknown. The weather was poor, but the west wind was behind her and helping her on, and she was confident of her ability to make the flight—provided the engine did not break down. Fortunately it was a new and thoroughly tested one, and there was ample fuel in the tanks. In the absence of really bad luck she felt confident she would succeed.

She was flying in the moonlight between two layers of cloud now, and the Atlantic below her was invisible. It was as though she were flying in some new element without reference to time or space, as though the familiar cockpit with its instru-ment panel, its controls and its equipment had nothing to do with the whole business, and as though she, Amelia Earhart, were a disembodied spirit.

Resolutely she pulled herself together and dismissed such fancies. Flyers on their own for long know them very well; for example, Lindbergh had experienced them on his Atlantic flight. She glanced at the altimeter. The needle pointed to zero. Something was obviously wrong with it. That was an unusual defect, but it might have been worse—it might have been something wrong with the engine. . . . Fortunately, that was running sweetly. On the other hand, it was a nuisance to have to do without the altimeter. It meant that when there was no visibility she might be much closer to the surface of the sea than she thought.

Just in case therefore she raised the nose of the Lockheed and went higher. Visibility was improving, and far down below the clouds she could make out the dark grey mass of the Atlantic just visible in the faint light of the moon. But at 23.30 hours all visibility ceased again and her plane flew into a violent storm. The only light now was provided by the frequent flashes of lightning, and the plane began to creak and groan under the hard buffetings of the wind. Amelia Earhart tried to go still higher in an effort to fly above the storm, but the plane rose only slowly and with difficulty.

'Icing,' she thought. 'I'll have to go down; but not too far. I can't see the surface, and without the altimeter I might go too low without noticing it—until it was too late!'

She went down lower, but the clouds were so thick that she was flying blind. That was uncomfortable, so she rose once more, and then the effects of icing began to make themselves felt again. It was a vicious circle. Fortunately she had a gyroscopic compass which enabled her to keep on her course without much difficulty. 'Without that, I should be lost,' she thought.

Then there was more trouble. For some time she had been mildly disturbed by the flames which were escaping from her exhaust pipe, but gradually the trouble grew worse. 'The metal's thick,' she thought, 'but will it last out all that time?'

She was feeling the loneliness a good deal now; that feeling of being utterly cut off from her kind, and without hope of aid if anything happened. 'Courage is the thing,' she told herself, 'all goes if courage goes.' And it was she who had said that women could try anything that men could dare. All the same, she would be very glad when it got light. But dawn seemed slow in coming. At last it did come through, lighting up the clouds and making those darting flames from the exhaust pipe look far less dangerous. Even apart from that, it seemed to her that they were no longer so fierce; the storm had diminished in violence, too.

Below her she could see the Atlantic, and she looked in vain for the sight of a ship. With a smile she remembered how she had bombed the *America* with oranges four years previously. She checked her course, and flew on through the rising sun, which was frequently blotted out by the wrack of the storm. The hours passed slowly and the engine kept up its steady throbbing. Midday; 14.00 hours; 16.00 hours. According to her calculations she must be approaching the Irish coast now, and she must certainly sight it before it grew dark again. Then she saw it ahead: the long, low-lying green earth of Ireland. She crossed the coast flying low and looking for a place to land, for her fuel was running out. Sighting a railway line she flew along it, knowing that it must ultimately lead her to some town; but when she came to it and flew around there was no aerodrome, as she had hoped.

Very well, she'd have to land in some suitable meadow. She spotted one that looked large enough and put the nose of her plane down to land there. Browsing cattle galloped away in all directions as the great bird soared down between them. Her wheels touched the ground, the plane bumped a little and then rolled forward heavily. The ground was soft, but fortunately the plane did not capsize. She clambered out of the cockpit, and her face, which had been drawn and tired, now lit up with a smile of relief. She had flown the Atlantic again—and this time not as a parcel. She knew already what she was going to say to the first person she met:

'I am Amelia Earhart, and I have just flown the Atlantic.'

14

A Record in Survival

IT was June 4th, 1932, and Stanley Haussner stared down at the Atlantic from his plane. He seemed to be looking at a great city of skyscrapers, and the deceptive light of the setting sun lit up and coloured their façades: black, grey, yellow, and dark red. The mirage extended for miles, and the geometrical skyline of this new capital of Atlantis stood out clearly against the sky.

'It can't be New York,' he muttered incredulously, and he knew he was talking nonsense, for New York was something like 2,500 miles behind him. And it really couldn't be any city in Europe. For one thing, Europe must lie another thousand miles or so ahead; for another, no European city had a skyline of skyscrapers like this one.

The lone flyer remembered the legend of St. Brendan. His island city was supposed to have emerged from the waves somewhere in mid-Atlantic. Haussner shrugged his shoulders. He was obviously seeing things. Other lone long-distance flyers had reported the same sort of thing. Not that he was likely to be able to confirm their reports, for he was alone in his plane about ten thousand feet over the Atlantic and over a thousand miles from land, and his tanks were almost empty. Within a very short time, with its propeller idly turning, his plane would soar down towards that greyish-green surface. And that would be the end of him and his machine, for darkness would soon be brooding over the Atlantic and there was not a ship in sight.

The day before encountering that mirage Stanley Haussner had taken off at dawn from New Jersey in an attempt to fly non-stop from the United States to Poland in the *Rose Marie*, a Bellanca plane not much bigger than the machine in which Lindbergh had made the Atlantic crossing a good many years previously.

For many years he had wanted to attempt the flight—as early as 1921, in fact, long before Lindbergh had set off. It had taken him over ten years to get together everything he wanted, but at dawn on June 3rd the moment had come. He had eaten his breakfast on the airfield with his wife and a few friends who had come to see him off. There had been coffee and eggs and bacon, but he had not eaten with any great appetite. Most of the time he had been looking out of the window at the mechanics putting the last touches to his machine as it stood there waiting for him on the tarmac.

The weather forecast was favourable. Once he had got round a trough of depression off Newfoundland there was every hope of good weather. His wife was pale but calm, and, obviously to give herself something to do, she carefully checked through the food he was taking with him on the flight: sandwiches, oranges, a bottle of tomato juice, a thermos flask of hot coffee, a bottle of mineral water. He knew her too well to be deceived: she was more nervy this time than she had been the previous week when he had taken off on his first attempt. After being in the air three hours he had had to turn back on account of engine trouble. When he smiled confidently at her from time to time her answering smile was a little forced.

When they had finished breakfast they rose, and Haussner went out to his machine. It was eight o'clock. The moderate head wind which had been forecast for that morning was blowing, and it was time to get away. He climbed into the cockpit of the *Rose Marie*, and the mechanics swung the propeller. He was about to give the signal for the take-off when through the cabin window he saw his wife running towards the machine with an anguished face. He opened the door of the cabin, climbed out, took her in his arms and kissed her again; then quickly disengaged himself, climbed back into the cockpit and gave the start signal. The mechanics removed the chocks, and the *Rose Marie* began her run. Before she had gone half-way along the runway she rose into the air with ease.

Haussner glanced at the revolution counter, and then throttled back to cruising speed. At about sixteen thousand feet he was running into grey clouds which became more and more dense over Cape Cod, and it began to rain. The worsening of the weather did not disturb him unduly; it was only the localized depression forecast by the weather experts. Within less than an hour it was behind him and the sky was clear again.

But it was raining again over Nova Scotia, and when he passed over Halifax the inhabitants thought that it was raining blue, yellow and red spots. But closer examination when they came down showed them to be leaflets with the message: 'Greetings on the New York, London, Warsaw flight. Stanley Haussner.' Haussner's plane had no wireless, and he dropped these leaflets to indicate his passage.

Showers of the same leaflets fell over Cape Breton and then over Newfoundland. Interested watchers stared up at the *Rose Marie* as she flew down low over the rooftops scattering her leaflets. Then she flew on, gaining altitude and disappearing out over the Atlantic at a height of 5,000 feet or so. The sky was sombre with many clouds, but towards the east the horizon was lightening as though to open the way to Europe to the intrepid flyer.

Haussner was calm and confident. A glance at the instrument panel showed him that the engine was doing 1,700 revolutions, or about 110 miles an hour. The sky was already dark now apart from a last trace or two of red on the horizon to the west. He was already beginning to experience that obsessive feeling of loneliness he had been warned about, but it did not disturb him unduly; in fact his loneliness seemed to protect him, to give him a paradoxical feeling of security.

Flight conditions were ideal now; visibility was good, an

there was only a slight head wind. Haussner was enjoying his own feelings of calmness and confidence. He had often tried to imagine just what it would feel like once he was well out over the Atlantic and completely on his own. He was afraid that he might experience misgivings at the thought that his life was completely at the mercy of an engine failure, or some other defect; that he might feel afraid of the unknown into which he was flying. But now he was facing it in reality he was not in the least disturbed or anxious. He was like a good workman calmly carrying out a task he knew by heart, and completely absorbed in it.

He didn't feel in the least tired, though he had been flying all day, and he was not particularly hungry either, but he decided to eat something, because he knew that the last part of the flight would be the most difficult—particularly as he was bound to get tired no matter how fresh he felt now. He ate a sandwich or two and drank some hot coffee, looking down with interest at the mass of the Atlantic below him as calmly and peacefully as a passenger on a transatlantic liner.

At 23.00 hours—it was quite dark—Haussner calculated the distance he had already flown: about fourteen hundred miles. At the same time he noticed that he had been flying slightly off course to the north, and he corrected his course by four degrees. He flew on calmly, almost mechanically. But at midnight he had to take a tighter hold on the controls, as the *Rose Marie* was caught in a sudden squall which shook her roughly and swiftly forced her down three hundred feet or so. Haussner regained control and took his plane up again, but a few minutes later the same thing happened, and he was astonished and a little alarmed at its violence. Once again he recovered control, took the *Rose Marie* up again, keeping a tight hand on the controls in the expectation of further squalls. But to his surprise and relief there were no more.

It was difficult to explain the reason for those two, so he contented himself with noting them in his log, and the fact that at the time the outer air temperature was 41° F. When he had finished these entries and had time to think of other things it struck him that somehow the atmosphere in the cabin was not quite the same, though what exactly was different about it he found it difficult to say. There was a smell of petrol, but so slight as to be unimportant. He checked all the dials on his instrument panel, and there was nothing there to disturb him.

He looked out. The visibility was not so good. The plane seemed to be flying through a slight mist. He looked to right and left, and found the sky clear, and yet ahead of him the windscreen was obscured by mist. That was odd. 'Some sort of condensation phenomenon,' he thought, and he ate an orange. However, the phenomenon persisted; it was as though fumes were rising in front of the windscreen. Now and again they were dispersed in the wind, but they always reappeared. Looking more closely Haussner noticed that from time to time his view was completely unobscured; then after a while those fumes were there again clinging to the pane.

He checked the speed of the wind, and found it unchanged. Casting around for some acceptable explanation of the strange phenomenon, he noticed with a shock that those fumes were inside the cabin now. Hurriedly he looked at the fuel gauge. The needle was moving in a fashion that suggested an irregular withdrawal. 'Choked somewhere,' he thought. 'That's why the engine's showing a tendency to overheat. Some impurity, perhaps. It'll shift on its own.'

He looked down, and there was a layer of nacreous cloud between him and the sea. As he stared it grew milky, almost phosphorescent. 'Daybreak!' he thought with relief. It was, in fact, the early dawn of June, for it was only 02.10 hours. His spirits rose considerably, as though the light would make an end of all his difficulties. The clouds were glowing pink like mountain tops now. Haussner blinked in the growing light and put on a pair of dark glasses. The fume-like phenomenon persisted, and he still racked his brain to find the explanation. This time he found it. It was in the vacuum-feed pipe which carried the petrol to the engine—it was obviously faulty. Haussner shut off the circulation and operated the pump which drew petrol from the wing tanks.

It was nothing serious, but it was fortunate that he had noticed it in time. He sighed in relief. Now that he had put the matter right he was almost glad that the thing had happened— at least he would not have done the flight without difficulty; to have overcome some material defect would enhance his achievement. He didn't want it to be too easy. Through a break in the cloud cover he saw the sea again. It was streaked with white foam and appeared to be very choppy. But it was so far away beneath him that it seemed difficult to believe that it was the one great enemy he had to overcome. Before long the gap closed and Haussner was alone in the clouds again.

He felt completely at peace now, and perfectly confident. The only danger was that he might fall asleep; to keep himself awake and his mind occupied he checked all his dials, noting his speed, his course, and his fuel reserves . . . His eyes widened and he felt the palms of his hands grow moist at what the fuel gauge told him. The needle indicator for the main fuel tank showed zero! 350 gallons in nineteen hours flying!

The defect in the vacuum-feed pipe was not enough to explain that. There must be some leak from the main tank. He made a rapid calculation. He had enough fuel left to keep his plane in the air for another twelve hours—another couple of hours on top of that in the best case. With a bit of luck that ought to be sufficient to get him to the Irish coast and safety. He took fuel-oil from his reserve tins, and filled up, but he was full of misgiving and he had a feeling of apprehension which was difficult to ignore.

He checked the pipes. The feed-pipe from the starboard wing tank seemed to be in order, but when he felt that of the port wing it was wet, and his hand was wet when he withdrew it. He smelt his fingers—it was fuel-oil all right. And then he knew what that second leak meant. No hope of making the Irish coast now. He would end in the sea. Just at that moment there was a further break in the cloud cover and he could see the Atlantic Ocean again, and a few floating icebergs. He could stay in the air for five or six hours, perhaps; no longer.

Had he anything to hope for? The nearest coastline was too far away to be reached. The chance of a ship? But he was too far north of the usual shipping lanes to have much hope of that. He had done about 2,500 miles so far, and now they seemed to string out behind him like a heavy chain, hampering him and preventing him from reaching the other shore. Mechanically he checked his course. It was correct, but he knew now that it would not lead him to Europe; it would end down below there in the Atlantic. For a while he continued to fly on course, but then resolutely he made his decision and turned southward towards the more frequented shipping lanes. That was his only hope, and the thought of his wife made him determined to take it. A continuation of his normal course could end only in death by drowning, alone and without hope of assistance; at least his present course might bring him aid. At first he had thought himself alone, but he was not; there were others: his wife, and the friends who had supported him so loyally in this venture.

He flew southward throughout the afternoon, but without sighting a ship of any kind. Then evening drew in and the sun began to set, and in his heart he feared that it would be the last he ever saw. It was then that he saw the mirage of that city of skyscrapers. Gradually it faded with the rays of the dying sun which had caused it.

He checked the fuel level. It was near zero. Now was the time to go down, whilst he still had power. He hoped to be able to set the *Rose Marie* down on the surface with the least possible damage. The altimeter indicated ten thousand feet, and he turned down the nose of his plane. At six thousand feet he was still surrounded by a clinging mist which robbed him of visibility. At three thousand feet, and then even at two thousand, he was still unable to see the surface. At a thousand feet he noticed that gulls were flying around, and then he saw the sea and looked around desperately in the hope of a miracle —a ship. But the Atlantic was empty in all directions.

He had perhaps enough fuel for another hour's flight, and he flew around in a great circle, hoping to spot a ship after all; but he was out of luck, and now he took his plane up again to gain height for the touching down. Suddenly the engine began to splutter; then it stopped, and the air-screw continued to turn idly in the wind. Whether he wanted to or not he had to go down now—down towards that vast greenish mass of water moving powerfully in a great foam-flecked swell. He was praying now, not for the sight of a ship—that was out of the question—he was just praying.

He knew, of course, that other flyers who had been forced down in the Atlantic from the days of Hawker and Mackenzie Grieve onwards, had been saved; but they had all been fortunate enough to come down within sight of a ship—and that was obviously just the difference between them and those many others who had never been heard of again. They, like him, had come down on an empty sea.

And as he descended he suddenly heard a slight hissing from his engine, and for a foolish moment he thought it was going to start up again—though what good would that have been? He hadn't enough fuel to take him to land, but it was like a drowning man clutching at a straw . . . A drowning man? And immediately he realized that it was the high-tossed spray of the breakers hissing against the still hot engine.

At least it did one good thing; it awakened the instinct of self-preservation, and brought him to himself with a jerk. Hurriedly he checked the watertightness of his cabin, shut all openings, noted the wind direction, and brought the *Rose Marie* down as lightly as possible parallel to and in the trough between two waves. The surface of the sea was very close now, and spray was already lashing against the cabin windows. Then a sudden shock told him that the *Rose Marie* had struck the water. The cabin filled immediately and the water rose over his head. Hurriedly he released himself from his safety belt and stood up. His head was above the surface, and he realized that although the *Rose Marie* was waterlogged she was floating and being carried up and down by the swell.

He pulled himself up and sat on the reserve tank. Various objects were floating around in the cabin, his books, his gloves, a cushion or two and a rug. He was saved for the time being, but for how long? Gradually the water level in the cabin would rise, and the *Rose Marie* would go under, taking him with her to be drowned like a rat in a trap. Not that it seemed to make much difference whether he was inside or outside the cabin when she went down, but desperately he wanted to get out of that cabin and be in the open air again.

But how? An exercise of all his strength on the side doors quickly showed that it was impossible to open them. The outside water pressure was too great. All that remained therefore was the roof, and seizing a heavy screwdriver he started to force up the top of the cabin. Of course, waves might break over it causing more water to flood into the cabin, which meant that the plane would sink with him in it; but as it was bound to do that ultimately, it was worth chancing, and he worked desperately. If he had to drown he preferred that it should be in the open sea with the free sky over his head.

It was hard work, and he seemed to make very slow progress, but at last he succeeded in forcing a hole, and soon it was big enough for him to stick his head out and look around. The horizon was sometimes near and sometimes far as the heavy swell lifted the machine up and dropped it back again into the trough between the waves; but far or near, one thing was quite certain—there was not a ship in sight, or the faintest smudge of smoke to be seen anywhere. Another thing was encouraging, though: the *Rose Marie* was not so deep in the water as he had feared. Perhaps two-thirds were out, and her tail was sticking up into the air while its fixed vertical plane was acting as a sail and carrying her along.

Gulls were wheeling around in the air above him. Sometimes they landed on the plane, perching on the tail and then flapping into the air again with a squawk. Somehow their presence comforted him; at least there was a sign of life. Now and again, too, he saw a fish. But when night fell, he was alone again, and there was not even anything illusory for his hope to cling to; nothing but darkness and emptiness and the sound of the moving sea. It was then that he had difficulty in not giving way to panic; and a sort of primitive terror of the darkness and loneliness swept over him. 'If I live to be a hundred I shall never forget the ordeal of that first night alone with my wrecked plane,' he was to say afterwards.

And, of course, there was another disadvantage of the night: he wouldn't be able to see a ship even if there were one, and the thought that a ship might pass within sighting distance, but be unable to see him because of the darkness, unnerved him. Once or twice during the night he thought he sighted faint lights at a distance, and he shouted wildly in the hope that he might be heard by some alert look-out. But whether they were the lights of ships, or even lights at all—they might have been the reflection of stars in the water—he never discovered. Perhaps it would have been better if he had tried to get some sleep, but this he could not bring himself to do; on the contrary, he fought tenaciously against sleep for fear that some ship might pass near enough to be hailed and he unable to see or hail her.

Before complete darkness had engulfed him and his plane he had managed to crawl out on to the roof of the cabin, and there he stayed, because it gave him a better chance of seeing anything that was to be seen. Once sleep did overcome him, but he woke up at once as he fell into the water. After that he stood up in the cabin with his head out of the hole. The swell was still long and heavy, and steadily it lifted the plane up and dropped her back again into the trough; as it raised her up Haussner stared desperately all around in the hope of sighting a ship. He was hungry as well as being tired now. It did not occur to him that even if he did spot a ship in the distance it would be very unlikely that he could attract the attention of anyone on board her, and that then his state would be worse than ever.

In fact this is precisely what happened to him the next day, and in broad daylight too. The heavy swell persisted, but the sky was clear and the horizon well defined. Then, towards midday, he was seized with wild excitement. There on the horizon away to the right was a black point. A ship? Now and again it disappeared, but always it reappeared again, and more clearly visible than before until finally there was no doubt about it: it was a ship!

He shouted the words aloud, as though to convince himself that it was true; and at the thought of what it meant to him— rescue from his water-logged prison, and a return to life—he scrambled out on to one wing, hurriedly pulled off his shirt and began to wave it wildly in the best castaway tradition, shouting for help at the top of his voice. It wasn't easy to keep his balance in the swell, and more than once he staggered and almost fell into the sea, but saved himself by clinging to a strut.

But it was all to no purpose. The ship's course did not come near enough to his plane for anyone on board to see him, and he had the mortification of watching it gradually pass and disappear in an easterly direction. For about an hour afterwards he could still see the trail of smoke it left behind on the horizon. What with hunger, fatigue and disappointment Haussner was almost at the end of his tether now, and he was greatly tempted to let himself fall into the sea and end it all that way; better a quick death by drowning than this. But then he climbed back into the cabin and sat there numbed until nightfall.

During the second night he made no attempt to keep watch. His experience with that distant ship during the day had convinced him that at night he stood no chance at all, and that it was a waste of time to try. It was clear that he could not last much longer. There was no food and no water, though at least the few supplies he had bought with him must be somewhere submerged in the cabin. He pulled himself together and decided to recover the food if he could, but his attempts were unsuccessful.

The next day, much cast down, he started his watch again. It was a warm day with a cloudy sky, but the visibility was fair. After a few hours he was more depressed than ever—not because he had seen no ships, but because they had all been in the distance and he had no means of drawing attention to his plight. Waving his shirt! It would be a keen-eyed look-out who could spot that at such a distance. He gave up in disgust and despair and went back into the water-logged cabin, trembling and unnerved.

The third night fell, and he did his best to sleep, stretched out on the reserve petrol tank. On one occasion he woke up with a start, fearing that the *Rose Marie* was sinking, but water-logged though she was she was still seaworthy and keeping above the waves. As far as he could see she had not settled down any deeper, and when daylight came he dived down to examine the floats to see whether they were still watertight. He found the air taps, and gently unscrewed them for a moment or two. Bubbles forced their way out at once, and he hastily screwed the taps up again as tightly as he could. Several times he had to surface to take in new air, and it was then he noticed that the plunge into the sea made him feel better. Satisfied that the floats of the *Rose Marie* were still watertight he clambered back into the cabin and decided to search for his provisions again. In particular he wanted the thermos of hot coffee, which he knew must be there somewhere.

After searching around under water for some time, coming up anew every few moments for air, he was tired out. All he managed to find was another screwdriver and a pair of pliers, which he now placed in safety above water level. They might come in useful. Then he climbed out of the cabin and on to one of the wings to start his watch again. The sea was calmer and there was not such a heavy swell. Thank goodness for that! The one thing that could end everything very quickly was an Atlantic storm; and storms were frequent enough in these parts. Despite his disappointments and his depression, Haussner still clung to life.

Whilst he was keeping his watch he spotted two dark points on the horizon to the left; and then after a while there were three. They looked to him like the tops of masts, and this they turned out to be when a stray wave lifted up the *Rose Marie* and enabled him to see farther. It was a three-masted steamship. Haussner climbed on to the top of the cabin and stood up to try and spot the ship's hull, but it was too far away. From their crow's nest a look-out might nevertheless see him, so he started to wave his shirt again, and to shout—sometimes a shout would carry very far in the silence, and the sea was making very little noise now.

But as the masts and funnel came in sight again and again, Haussner was forced to realize with a sinking heart that the ship was not coming any closer; then he saw that she was gradually receding. Half an hour later the horizon was empty again. Each time he suffered such a disappointment he felt more and more depressed, but then he pulled himself together. After all, although no one had sighted him so far, the frequent appearance of ships showed that he had come down in the frequented sea lanes, and there was every hope that sooner or later—if the weather stayed fine and the *Rose Marie* stayed afloat—some ship would come near enough to spot him.

The thought raised his spirits again; but if he were to be found it would have to be soon, for he was suffering very greatly now from hunger and, in particular, from thirst—he had been unable, despite repeated attempts, to find that thermos flask with the coffee. Then he remembered that there was an untouched bottle of mineral water there somewhere too, and once again he scrabbled around under water in the cabin. This time he was luckier, and with a bounding heart his fingers closed round the bottle, but when he rose above the surface with it he found to his tremendous disappointment that the top had come off the bottle and that its contents were brackish.

In addition to the thermos flask there was also a tin of

tomato juice; that at least must still be watertight. He went under again, and kept on trying. After he had tried seven times again all he had brought to the surface was a few sodden cushions and his charts, but no tomato juice and no coffee.

The funny thing, was, however, that despite his hunger and thirst he felt better. For one thing his hopes were still high; at some time or other a ship was bound to find him—if the *Rose Marie* stayed afloat. Then it occurred to him that her wings, which were damaged and attached to her stern only by wires, would be better discarded, particularly as the movement of the swell was rasping them against the fuselage and might well cause the cabin to spring a leak. So with screwdriver and pliers he set to work, and before long he had got rid of one of the wings. It floated off on its own.

He was making good progress with the other wing when he suddenly had the impression that something dark had passed beneath him. At first he thought he must have been mistaken, but then it happened again. Suddenly he realized that it was a shark, and he started back with an involuntary shout of horror to take refuge on the fuselage.

For two hours after that the shark swam around in the neighbourhood of the waterlogged *Rose Marie*, and Haussner squatted on the top of her cabin and watched it. It was a danger he hadn't thought of—perhaps after all it would be better to go down, if he had to go down, inside the cabin. Then the brute disappeared.

That night Haussner was troubled with nightmares, dreams that were so real that when he woke up it was difficult to believe that he had been dreaming. In one of them he climbed out of the cabin and found a man removing the plugs from the engine. It was the mechanic who had checked the engine before the flight—but when Haussner protested that the plugs were all right, the fellow just grinned wider and wider and disappeared in the gaping hole. Then he saw his wife, his mother and his friends, and they all promised him food and drink. 'And don't forget fuel-oil,' he said. 'That's what I need to get away from here.' His mother was still there after the others had disappeared, and she was preparing him an orange: 'Drink this juice, Stanley. It will do you good . . . It will do you good . . . It will do you good . . .'

And the words turned into the murmur of the sea as he woke up at dawn. He climbed out on to the roof of the cabin, and then he saw a steamer. It was nearer than any of the others had been. He could see its hull and its plimsoll line, and even the white lettering of its name, though without being able to read it. This time they must see him! Once again he began to wave his shirt and to shout for help. Then he was overjoyed to see that the ship was slowing down. But so slowly! After a while he realized that it was not slowing down at all, but moving away farther and farther from him. For a moment or two he was tempted to plunge into the sea and swim for it, but he was still lucid enough to realize that it would be certain death, so silently he stood there and watched the unknown ship disappearing in the distance.

It was difficult to tell how long he stood there numbed and downcast. Time had almost ceased to have any meaning for him; it was not until it began to grow dark that he became conscious of himself again. On the horizon to the south-west he could see a liner, but this time it aroused no surge of hope in him; he had been disappointed too often. Then he saw that it actually was coming closer. There were already lights on board, though the sun had not yet sunk beneath the horizon and still showed up the ship's contours very clearly. He began to shout again. His voice seemed loud in the silence of the evening, and he felt sure that he would be heard on board. This time the look-out must spot him and his plane!

But despite all the shouting and waving, the liner steamed past and then disappeared as all the other ships had disappeared. Within half an hour what Haussner now felt to have been his last hope, had gone. He was too depressed to climb back into the cabin and lie down on the fuel tank, and instead he stretched himself out on top of the cabin and tried to sleep, careless of the danger of rolling off into the water. Above him dark clouds were moving across the sky, and he wondered whether it was going to rain.

Another night passed, and when dawn broke the surface of the sea was still empty but for the fin of a shark or two as it cut through the water. As he watched those fins it occurred to him that they were probably attracted by a shoal of fish in the neighbourhood.

He made himself a line, using a piece of bent wire as a hook baited with a small piece of flesh which he tore from a wound on his hand sustained when falling violently against one corner of the reserve tank. Then he tried to fish, but he found himself growing so giddy that he had to give it up before he could catch anything. He was growing weaker now, and some of the time he was delirious; so he lay on his side and looked out towards the horizon, though more and more often his eyes grew so blurred that he couldn't see.

Then he saw another ship. It was bearing down on him from the north-east, but the sight of it was no longer enough to excite him, though it was not more than a mile away at the utmost. 'It will pass without seeing me just as all the others did,' he thought. 'Let it.' In fact he was not even sure that the approaching vessel was real at all; perhaps it was one of the many hallucinations from which he was beginning to suffer increasingly. But the ship came nearer; near enough for him to distinguish the faces of men on board. Then he heard shouts, and he pulled himself together; at least that was a form of illusion he had not yet suffered from. Someone was hailing him. And then there was the harsh, screeching sound of davits, followed by a splash as a lifeboat hit the water. It was released, and the men in it pulled vigorously towards the *Rose Marie*.

They were men of the *Circe Shell*, and they took him into their boat and rowed him back to their ship, but by this time he was completely delirious and unaware that what he had longed for was now a reality. He was saved.

It was 19.00 hours on June 11th, and six hundred miles from

the coast of France. Stanley Haussner had survived in the waterlogged wreck of the *Rose Marie* for seven days, and had been picked up at last.

'And what are you going to do now, Mr. Haussner?' asked a reporter when Stanley Haussner stepped ashore on his return to the United States. 'I dare say you've had enough of transatlantic flying.'

'Not at all,' he replied firmly. 'I shall try again. I seem to bear a charmed life, and next time I shall succeed.'

But the courageous Stanley Haussner was wrong. In the following year, when he was making a test flight with the new machine with which he intended to carry out his original intention, he crashed and was killed.

15

The Final Operations

Costes and Bellonte had succeeded magnificently in their east–west flight across the Atlantic, but their great experience and ability as airmen, and the careful preparations and the long period of waiting they had considered necessary, all underlined the difficulties and dangers which still attached to any transatlantic flight. In 1930 Jean Mermoz had made the first commercial crossing of the South Atlantic, but it was clear that there was a long way to go before commercial and air-mail flights over the North Atlantic could become a regular service. Opinion now began to veer back to the hydroplane, or the more advanced flying-boat, as perhaps the best instrument for the job after all.

In 1928 the British flyer Courtney took off with a Dornier-Wal flying-boat and a crew of three. He reached the Azores without much difficulty, but there he was immobilized for a month by bad weather, and he did not take off again until August 2nd, making for Newfoundland. When they had flown about five hundred miles fire broke out and the Dornier had to come down in the sea. Courtney and his men succeeded in putting out the flames, but the flying-boat was now a charred wreck drifting in the darkness. But at least their wireless was still in order, and the S.S. *Minnewaka* picked up their S.O.S. and steamed to the spot. Courtney and his crew were taken safely on board.

The very same day on which they were picked up another Dornier flying-boat had to turn back over the Atlantic. It was piloted by Franco, the man who had succeeded in crossing the

South Atlantic by stages in 1926. This time he was engaged on a flight round the world, but engine trouble forced him to put about and return to Spain.

The following year he tried again—not to fly round the world this time, but to fly non-stop from Carthagena to New York. On June 21st he was on his way to the Azores, and a despatch duly arrived reporting his arrival at San Miguel. The exact time of the touch-down was given: 08.22 hours. But the report remained unconfirmed and was subsequently denied. Franco and his flying-boat had not arrived, and the astonishing thing was that no wireless message from him had been picked up.

It began to look as though transatlantic flying had claimed more victims. Just as was the case after the disappearance of Nungesser and Coli, a variety of hopeful but false reports began to come in: a British steamer had come across the wrecked plane and rescued the crew; fishermen had heard the sound of a plane in the air; a Swedish vessel reported having sighted a plane in the sea; the captain of another vessel announced that he had heard a plane flying round and round above him in the darkness.

In the meantime a squadron of Spanish destroyers was searching the area with the assistance of French destroyers, whilst the British aircraft-carrier H.M.S. *Eagle* put out from Gibraltar to take part in the search. On June 29th the Spanish dictator, Primo de Rivera, made a statement to journalists from which it was clear that the Spanish authorities feared the worst. The planes of H.M.S. *Eagle* had returned from all their flights with nothing to report, and the search was reluctantly abandoned. Franco and his men were given up for lost.

But at dawn on June 29th the officer of the watch on board H.M.S *Eagle* thought he saw rocket signals in the distance, and soon half a dozen pairs of sea glasses were concentrated on the spot. It was a miracle, but no mirage. H.M.S. *Eagle* steamed hurriedly to the spot and picked up Franco and his men, safe and sound. They had been drifting in the sea in their

flying-boat for a week. As their wireless had broken down it
had been impossible for them to let anyone know of their
plight.

The French tried with flying-boats too, but their efforts
were dogged with bad luck. Lieut.-Comdr. Paris started out
on a flight to New York, and reached the Azores on July 23rd,
1928, but there he had to give up. The well-known French
flyer Gilbaud was about to attempt a flight to New York from
Europe, but he postponed it in order to take his flying-boat
to the Arctic Circle to join in the search for the Italian airship
commander General Nobile, whose airship the *Italia* was
reported lost on the return flight from the North Pole. Gilbaud
picked up the famous Norwegian explorer Amundsen in
Tromsø, and his Latham flying-boat set off with a crew of
three on board. For a while wireless touch was maintained and
then it ceased. One of the greatest tragedies of flying had
occurred—in their efforts to rescue Nobile, Amundsen and
the three French flyers had lost their lives.

The Germans, great believers in the flying-boat, were busy
too. In 1930 von Gronau flew in stages from Germany to
America via Iceland and Greenland in his Dornier-Wal, a
little before the flight of Costes and Bellonte. And on
November 5th of the same year the Dornier Company sent out
the Do-X, a giant flying-boat with twelve engines, to fly by
stages from Germany to South America, which it did quite
successfully though it was considerably delayed by various
difficulties. Then it flew up to New York. The return flight
was much quicker, and taking off on May 19th the great flying
boat touched down off Spain on May 22nd.

The Italian Fascist General Balbo was another believer in
the usefulness of flying-boats. He set off with a squadron of
fourteen across the South Atlantic, and eleven of his machines
arrived in Natal without having suffered breakdowns; and in
July and August, 1933, he made a similar formation flight
over the North Atlantic via Iceland and Labrador, returning
via Newfoundland and the Azores.

But these achievements, remarkable as they were, did not solve the problem of regular commercial transatlantic flights. The aeroplane was much faster than the flying-boat, but as against that it was less safe in the event of engine trouble. On the other hand, the flying-boat was much slower, and had the further disadvantage that it was very often difficult to get it to take-off at all.

The giant airship was not out of the reckoning, even now, and it was by no means certain that Wellman, the first pioneer, had not been right, particularly as the giant airship *Graf Zeppelin*, 775 feet long and with a capacity of 3,708,600 cubic feet, had actually flown across the Atlantic on October 11th, 1928, with a crew of thirty-seven men under the command of Dr. Hugo Eckener, carrying eighteen passengers and air-mail. The crossing was not an easy one, however; it took 111 hours and was constantly delayed by bad weather which caused a certain amount of damage to the structure. The return flight was more successful and took only seventy-five hours.

In 1929, with a view to demonstrating the qualities of his airship to the world, Dr. Eckener started off on a world tour, flying across both the Atlantic and the Pacific Oceans, 21,700 miles in 20 days 4 hours. In 1930 he flew over seventy thousand miles with his Zeppelin, and in 1931 he made three flights from Germany to South America and back successfully.

In view of these highly efficient and satisfactory performances it began to look very much as though, for the time being at least, the given instrument for commercial and air-mail transatlantic flying was the airship. Of course, even in the most favourable conditions it was by no means as fast as the aeroplane, or even the flying-boat, but as against that it was safer and more reliable. But then two terrible disasters abruptly faced the world with the sudden dangers that were possible in dirigible flying.

On October 5th, 1930, the British dirigible R-101, a steel-girder construction powered by Diesel engines, set off for a flight to Karachi, but crashed in a storm at Beauvais in France, bursting into flames. There were few survivors, and 47 people were killed, including Lord Thomson, the Air Minister. As a result of this disaster the British Government scrapped its other big airship R-100 and abandoned its airship programme indefinitely.

On April 4th, 1933, the U.S. airship *Akron*, named after the airship with which Vaniman had unsuccessfully attempted to fly the Atlantic in 1912, crashed into the sea off the New Jersey coast with the loss of seventy-three officers and men. And on February 12th, 1935, her sister-ship the *Macon* was returning from fleet manœuvres when flying control was lost and the airship settled into the sea. This time only two lives were lost, but it gave a further dampener to American enthusiasm for the rigid dirigible.

The Germans, with their usual persistence, carried on with the construction of giant airships, and their biggest was the Zeppelin *Hindenburg* with a capacity of 7,063,000 cubic feet. With this airship they actually operated the first commercial air service across the Atlantic. She carried 1,002 passengers on a total of ten trips to and fro, making eastbound crossings in an average time of 65 hours, and westbound crossings in an average time of 52 hours. But on May 6th, 1937, whilst landing at Lakehurst, New Jersey, on the first trip of the 1937 trans-atlantic flying season, she suddenly burst into flames and was completely destroyed with the loss of 36 lives.

A sister-ship, again named the *Graf Zeppelin*, was constructed and adapted for use with helium gas, which is non-inflammable, and therefore the answer to the terrible danger of fire on board. She was ready for commercial transatlantic flying in 1938, but it proved impossible to obtain the helium gas required, and the proposed service was abandoned. The outbreak of war in 1939 put an end to German airship activity, and it has not been resumed since.

Whilst the first *Graf Zeppelin* was flying across the Atlantic, apparently in perfect safety, the pilots of heavier-than-air

machines continued to risk their lives in attempting exploits
not all of which were of any real service to the cause of flying.
For example, on October 17th, 1928, Lieutenant MacDonald
made an attempt to fly the Atlantic from east to west in a light
aeroplane with one engine of 80 h.p. Nothing was ever heard
of him or his plane after it had disappeared from sight over
the Atlantic. Two years later, two Germans named Hirth and
Waller set off in another light plane with the intention of
reaching Chicago by stages. They got as far as Iceland and
then gave up.

But more serious attempts were still being made, and on
June 23rd, 1931, Wiley Post and Harold Gatty set off from
New York to fly round the world back to New York via
Newfoundland, Great Britain, Russia and the Pacific. They
arrived back in New York on July 1st, having flown 15,500
miles in eight days.

Endresz and Magyar took off from Newfoundland on
July 13th of the same year, and made the non-stop crossing to
land in Hungary; and on July 28th Russell N. Boardman and
John Polando flew non-stop from Bennett Field in New York
to Istanbul, arriving on the 30th after having covered 5,011
miles in 49 hours and 20 minutes.

All these were outstanding performances, but they still had
a record-breaking air about them, and the sporting interest was
still greater than the practical. The ultimate aim of a regular
passenger and mail service across the Atlantic was still a matter
of the future. But someone believed that passenger carrying
was already a possibility, and that was a certain Major
Hutchinson, who decided in the following year, 1932, that he
would fly with his wife and his two children from America to
Europe.

They took off in a hydroplane aptly named the *Flying
Family*, and before starting they were interviewed by reporters.
Major Hutchinson declared that he was quite confident of
success, and that his two children, six years and eight years old
respectively, would be the first children to fly across the

Atlantic. Major Hutchinson had not chosen the direct route, but the one to the north; nevertheless the experts were very doubtful of the whole undertaking. The Hutchinsons arrived safely in Newfoundland, and on August 25th they were off Anticosti Island in the Gulf of St. Lawrence. From there they flew to Labrador and then to Greenland. But on September 11th a message from the *Flying Family* was picked up in the Danish colony of Angmagssalik, reporting that the plane had come down in the sea about thirty miles from the coast on account of engine trouble, and that help was needed.

The weather was still good, and a number of fishing vessels happened to be in the neighbourhood—including the trawler *Lord Talbot*, which was about twenty-five miles away from the position given by Major Hutchinson. The skipper of the *Lord Talbot* steamed as fast as he could to the spot, and arrived there in the evening, but could find no trace of the *Flying Family*. Apart from a few icebergs the sea was empty. This was disappointing, but he was not so easily discouraged. Even assuming that the original position given was correct, the wind and the tide might well have carried the hydroplane away out of sight, so he steamed in the general direction in which, according to his calculations, the plane would have drifted. In the meantime no further messages were being received, but even that the gallant skipper found not too depressing. After all, their wireless might have broken down; that sort of thing often happened, so he continued his search.

Other vessels were joining in now, but none of them met with any greater success. The famous German flying ace Udet happened to be within reach, and he flew to the area to take part in the search, but even with his very much greater range he was unable to find anything. Forty hours had now passed since that first message of distress had been picked up, and it began to look as though the Hutchinson family had gone under. But with the thought of those two children in mind the searchers kept on grimly.

On the morning of the third day of the search when the *Lord*

Talbot was in sight of land, the look-out reported smoke on shore, probably from a fire. At first it was thought to be an Eskimo encampment, and the skipper of the *Lord Talbot* trained his glasses on to the spot. As they came closer he could distinguish the fire and a great pile of wood. Near by was what looked like some sort of vessel. There were one or two figures in the neighbourhood too. He felt quite sure they were Eskimos, but fortunately he decided to put in and inquire whether they had seen anything of a plane in the neighbourhood.

And then it struck him that two of the figures he could see were much smaller than the others. 'Eskimos don't take their children with them on fishing expeditions,' he thought. 'I wonder . . .' He continued to put the head of the *Lord Talbot* in to the shore, threading his way through the pack ice, and steaming round icebergs. One of them robbed him of all sight of the spot for a while, but when the *Lord Talbot* came within sight of the supposed Eskimo encampment again, very much closer, her skipper saw through his glasses that his search was over. What he had taken to be some sort of a vessel was the *Flying Family* lying wrecked inshore, and the figures were those of Major Hutchinson and his wife and their two children. The 'flying family' were saved.

Major Hutchinson did not have a very good press for his performance; the thought of those two children who had nearly lost their lives made an unfavourable impression; and more than one voice was raised to express the hope that the whole regrettable affair would serve as a warning to others that Atlantic flying was still a highly dangerous and chancy business. But this hope proved unfounded.

On September 13th, when the repercussions of the Hutchinson affair had hardly died away, American reporters and cameramen found themselves surrounding further candidates for a transatlantic flight. They questioned the pilot, whose name was Ulrich.

'I am flying from New York to Rome with two passengers,'

he declared. 'Dr. Pisculli and Miss Newcomer, a nurse, are coming with me.'

'What's the idea?' demanded the reporters.

'Dr. Pisculli is anxious to study the reactions of the human organism on a long flight. Miss Newcomer has volunteered to be under observation. When we reach Florence she will land by parachute.'

Even the hard-boiled American newspapermen were almost speechless at this foolery, which, in fact, turned into tragedy.

The *American Nurse*, as the plane was called, was last heard of about 250 miles off the coast of Spain. A search proved in vain, and the world never had the benefit of Dr. Pisculli's observations.

16

Ultimate Victory

ON August 5th, 1933, a Blériot plane with a 500 h.p. Hispano engine was wheeled on to the runway at Bennett Field in New York—named after the famous American flyer and friend and companion of Commander Byrd, Floyd Bennett. The two flyers this time were Codos and Rossi, a very different team from some of the others who had recently attempted to defeat the Atlantic.

The *Joseph Le Brix*, as the plane was called in memory of another great French flyer, started its run, but Codos had great difficulty in getting it off the ground with its great weight of fuel; for a moment or two the spectators thought that it would end in the sea, but Codos managed to get the nine tons weight off the ground, shaved the masts of a ship and then rose into the air on its way across the Atlantic.

Before long they ran into a violent storm, and Codos had all he could do to keep control of the pitching, rolling machine, but by nightfall the weather improved, and the *Joseph Le Brix* flew on well above the clouds. On the way they had trouble with icing, and for one period they were in considerable danger, but in the end they overcame all their difficulties and on the morning of the second day they sighted the French coast. A little later Paris came into view.

Paris was not their objective, for they were out to set up a new long-distance flying record. They flew low over Le Bourget and dropped messages on the airfield there, then regained height and continued their flight: Strasbourg, Vienna, and south across the Ægean Sea to the island of

Rhodes. The second night in the air was very difficult, for by this time the two flyers were very, very tired and nearing exhaustion—to such an extent in fact that they both suffered from hallucinations. The following evening they landed at Rayak in Syria, having gone considerably beyond the island of Rhodes.

They had certainly broken the long-distance flying record, having flown 5,657 miles non-stop in 55 hours. But Codos now wanted to do the return journey; he had done the west–east crossing on the Lindbergh route, and now he wanted to do the east–west crossing on the Costes–Bellonte route.

On May 27th, 1934, the *Joseph Le Brix* took the air again, loaded with fuel. Not surprisingly, the take-off presented some difficulties this time too, for there was a total weight of ten tons to be got off the ground, but once again Codos managed it, though he only just scraped over a line of trees bordering the airfield at Le Bourget. This time the flight was to take them east–west to Newfoundland, south–west to New York, and then west again to San Francisco right across the American continent.

During the night flying conditions were ideal, but at dawn off Newfoundland they suddenly worsened. A high wind sprang up, and the *Joseph Le Brix* was rudely buffeted. There was nothing extraordinary about this, but a phenomenon which neither of the flyers could understand was the violent way in which the whole plane was shuddering and vibrating. They did their best to discover the cause, but they could find nothing; the engine was certainly running perfectly smoothly. But the thing was very disquieting and they adjusted their parachutes—just in case.

Over Newfoundland they were sorely tempted to make a landing, but the engine was still running sweetly and the plane was under control, so they decided to continue their flight. But when they came in sight of New York the strange vibrations were still troubling them, and they decided that they had challenged the fates sufficiently, so they abandoned the rest of the flight across the United States and touched down in New York on Bennett Field, having flown 4,000 miles in 38 hours 27 minutes; a very fine performance, but not the record-breaker they had intended.

With the assistance of U.S. mechanics they went over their machine in an effort to find what was wrong. The first thing they found was damage to the propeller: the metal sheathing of one of the blades had been ripped up. Codos was puzzled, neither the wind nor the hail could have done that. And then, jammed in their undercarriage, they found a large branch of a tree. It was this which had upset the aerodynamic flow and caused those vibrations. At first the two flyers were flabbergasted, but then they remembered that line of trees bordering Le Bourget airfield. They had thought that they had safely surmounted them, but obviously the propeller had hit one of them whilst the undercarriage had torn away a branch. They realized that only by a miracle of inches had they escaped disaster.

The two flyers next turned their attention to the South Atlantic, and on January 16th, 1935, they took off in the *Joseph Le Brix* from Istres in Provence to fly to Natal in Brazil. But off the north-west coast of Africa they ran into trouble: a defective fuel-pipe, the very thing which had beaten the *Comte de Vaulx* and Jean Mermoz in more or less the same area.

'Think of your own safety first, and don't hesitate to sacrifice the plane if necessary,' were the orders given to them by General Denain, the French Air Minister.

But Codos and Rossi were very unwilling to lose the gallant *Joseph Le Brix* which had already served them so well, and they determined to do their utmost to reach the Cape Verde Islands. Ships *en route* were informed, and some of them changed course to be on hand in case of trouble. The further progress of the flyers was followed with anxiety, but all went well in the end, and Codos succeeded in landing the *Joseph Le Brix* safely at Porto Praya—with not a drop of fuel left in the tanks.

The long-distance flights of Codos and Rossi marked the

end of the heroic stage of transatlantic flying; the era of regular commercial services was approaching at last. The Americans set up an intermediate base in the Azores, and in 1936 a Lockheed Electra plane made an experimental to-and-fro flight across the Atlantic successfully. The Germans stationed ships at sea to serve the same purpose for the flying-boats of the Lufthansa. At the same time one of their four-engined Condors flew from Berlin to New York non-stop, and then back again non-stop in a total of three days thirteen hours.

On July 5th, 1937, the U.S. flying-boat *Clipper III* flew from Newfoundland to Ireland carrying mail, whilst at the same time the British flying-boat *Caledonia* was carrying mail in the opposite direction. The commercial air-crossing on the Atlantic was now becoming a reality, though as yet it had not taken on its final form.

In France, Codos, who was now Inspector-General of Air-France, firmly believed that the aeroplane was a better instrument for transatlantic flying than the flying-boat; in his opinion the future would belong to land planes flying at great heights beyond the reach of atmospheric disturbances, machines with pressurized passenger cabins along the lines of those already in use aboard the Boeing Stratocruisers flying American air lines in the interior. He succeeded in getting his point of view accepted, and three planes were specially built: the *Flammarion*, the *Leverrier* and the *Jules Verne*. Unfortunately the outbreak of the Second World War put an end for the time being to the plans for commercial transatlantic flying and the three great planes were put to very different uses. The *Flammarion* was used to combat German raiders over the Atlantic shipping routes; in June, 1940, the *Jules Verne* was the first plane to bomb Berlin; and the *Leverrier* was shot down in flames by enemy fighters over the Mediterranean. Two famous French pilots, Guillaumet and Reine, lost their lives, together with a well-known passenger—the former Paris Prefect of Police, the little Corsican Chiappe, who was on his way to Syria.

Commercial air-mail and passenger services were started in 1945 immediately after the war. At first they followed the Alcock–Brown route, and not the routes of Lindbergh and Costes and Bellonte, but before long the other routes were to come also. By 1947 Constellations were flying the direct route from Paris to New York and New York to Paris, and so on.

What those early aeronauts and flyers had set out to do had been done at last: the Atlantic Ocean had been conquered.